ENDORSEMENTS

For many years, Garth Black's name has been synonymous with a special interest and understanding about the nature, work, and influence of the Holy Spirit. This book is an excellent choice for adult Bible classes in any congregation, for small group discussion, and for individual study. Such use would not only help clarify vague ideas about the Holy Spirit, but will serve as a source of strength and edification for each person.

Dr. Earle West
Professor of Education, Retired Howard
University Washington, D.C.

Over thirty years ago, I was searching for a book on the Holy Spirit to help me teach students in a Bible study group. I ran across a book by Garth Black on the Holy Spirit. It was just what I wanted. I was disappointed when it went out of print and I could no longer purchase it for my students. When I read his new book I was greatly impressed. I believe the changes he has made have made it even better for both laymen and clergy to understand the Bible's teaching on the Holy Spirit.

I highly recommend this book and pray it will be a blessing to everyone that decides to read it. Furthermore, I sincerely thank Garth Black for taking the time to update and expand his earlier work. I say this because good, Biblically based books on the Holy Spirit are difficult to find. I judge this book to be one of the best books on the subject available today.

Dan Groghan
Senior Engineer Fulcrum Corporation
Arlington, VA

For centuries, Christians seeking a deeper understanding of and a relationship with the Holy Spirit have sought answers through the church, but have received confusing or contradictory teachings or no teaching at all. They long to understand and experience the Holy Spirit. They love to have fellowship with God. Yet churches continue to sideline the subject, leaving young people to search for understanding elsewhere.

Garth Black has spent his life as a serious student of scripture uncovering the deepest truths of the Holy Spirit. In this volume, he provides an inspirational, yet practical guide for understanding the role of the Holy Spirit in the life of the Christian. I challenge any reader to come away from reading this book without a great sense of awe and gratitude for the tremendous gift God has given his children.

Rick Gibson
Vice President for Public Affairs and
Church Relations Pepperdine University.

EMPOWERED
by the GRACE
of GOD

A Study of the Holy Spirit in the
Life of the Christian

EMPOWERED
by the GRACE
of GOD

GARTH W. BLACK

TATE PUBLISHING
AND ENTERPRISES, LLC

Published by Tate Publishing & Enterprises, LLC
127 E. Trade Center Terrace | Mustang, Oklahoma 73064 USA
1.888.361.9473 | www.tatepublishing.com

Tate Publishing is committed to excellence in the publishing industry. The company reflects the philosophy established by the founders, based on Psalm 68:11,
"The Lord gave the word and great was the company of those who published it."

Book design copyright © 2014 by Tate Publishing, LLC. All rights reserved.
Cover design by Joana Quilantang
Interior design by Jimmy Sevilleno

Published in the United States of America

ISBN: 978-1-63418-805-0
1. Religion / Christianity / Holy Spirit
2. Religion / Biblical Studies / Bible Study Guides
14.10.03

To my wife of sixty-four years,
Doris M. Black

ACKNOWLEDGEMENTS

FIRST AND FOREMOST, I express my gratitude to my wife, Doris, for her computer skills and editorial ability. This book would not have been possible without her assistance.

I wish to thank Don Groghan, for transcribing my previous book on to a CD. This was a huge help in writing this book. My thanks to Paige Talley, for transcribing a number of my speeches on the Holy Spirit into a written format. Her work benefited my organizing and writing process greatly.

I thank Dr. Earle West, a friend for over forty-five years, for his encouragement and for writing the foreword for this book.

I wish to express my lifelong gratitude to two of my professors and mentors who had a profound influence on my understanding of Scripture. The late Dr. Frank Pack, professor of Bible at Abilene Christian University and

Pepperdine University and the late Dr. J. D. Thomas, former head of the Bible Department at Abilene Christian
University. These two men had a powerful impact on my
scriptural knowledge and subsequent preaching for the past
sixty years. In 1956, Dr. Pack suggested I write my master's
thesis on "The Holy Spirit in the Life of a Christian." As
a result of that suggestion, I have written two books and
presented many lectures on that subject. That "small" suggestion has been life-changing for me. I am forever in his
and Dr. Thomas's debt.

CONTENTS

FOREWORD

PROBABLY YOU AND I share with other Christians a feeling that we have a fair grasp of the doctrine of God the Father as creator and of Jesus Christ, the Son, in his redemptive role. But for many of us, the Holy Spirit is a vague entity, which we know is often mentioned in Scripture but whose nature is thought to range from an impersonal thing equated with the words of Scripture or some better-felt-than-told inner feeling.

This confusion is compounded when we read in some translations the term *Holy Ghost*. We wonder what is *He* or *It* and how the Holy Spirit affects us as Christians. Readers of this book will have a sense of satisfaction regarding these questions after working through the book, even though God in his eternal majesty will never be fully grasped by human beings. Garth Black argues that neither of these two extremes is consistent with biblical teaching. His explanations are clear and strongly grounded with biblical references.

Readers at every level will find this material understandable without special theological training and will also appreciate the scope of the discussion. This book would be an excellent choice for adult Bible classes in any congregation, for small group discussions, and for individual study. Such use would not only help clarify vague ideas about the Holy Spirit but would also serve as a source of spiritual strength and edification for each person.

For many years, the name Garth Black has been synonymous with a special interest and understanding about the nature, work, and influence of the Holy Spirit. His scholarship was first demonstrated in a master's thesis from Abilene Christian College (now University). Later, it was put into a widely used adult class workbook published by ACU Press. This has been out of print for several years, but the value of the material led to continued requests for copies.

During his tenure as pulpit minister for the Silver Spring (Maryland) Church of Christ, Garth preached and taught classes on this topic. Some years later, he returned for a weekend series of lectures on "The Holy Spirit in the Life of the Christian," which was well-received. He has given special lectures in other places over the years. This book is the result of years of study, revising, and rethinking the biblical doctrine of the Holy Spirit in which we can all now profitably share.

—Earle H. West, Ph.D.
Professor of Education (Ret.)
Howard University
Washington DC

INTRODUCTION

ONE REASON FOR writing this book is best understood by an incident, which occurred when I was studying with a young man in the US Air Force. After several sessions, we began to study the subject of forgiveness. He had a reservation, however, and said, "I would like to be a Christian, but I don't believe I can live up to the standard necessary to live a Christian life. Why even begin? I know I will fail, so why even start?"

I explained to him that there are two concepts he failed to grasp. First, after being forgiven by God, we are continuously forgiven through the grace of God as we seek to love Him and follow Him. There will be times we fail, but God will forgive. Forgiveness is not based on performance, but on our possessing a proper attitude toward God and a sincere effort to obey and serve Him.

Secondly, the young man needed to understand the role of the Holy Spirit, which God gives him the moment he is forgiven by God's grace. The Holy Spirit will guide and encourage him through the Word of God, and the Holy Spirit will actually dwell within him to provide comfort, assurance, and confidence of his salvation. The Spirit will also provide strength to resist temptation and the power of Satan. The Holy Spirit serves as an intercessor on his behalf before the throne of God. I assured him that God will be with him through the Holy Spirit to help him serve God and his fellowmen, live the Christian life, and bear the fruit of the Spirit. Joyfully, I report that he became a Christian, giving his life to God.

It is the purpose of this study to look briefly at the work of the Holy Spirit in the Old Testament and in the life and teaching of Jesus. The main emphasis will be on the work and activity of the Holy Spirit in the life of Christians. Christianity is the age of the Holy Spirit, and the greatest emphasis in the New Testament is the work of the Holy Spirit as a comforter and intercessor and as a source of knowledge, inspiration, motivation, strength, and power in the daily lives of Christians. These areas of His work will be the major emphasis of this book.

The doctrine of the Holy Spirit, His personality, His work, and His relationship to God and man is clearly taught within God's written Word. The Holy Spirit is a central figure in both the Old and New Testaments. There are eighty-eight references in the Old Testament to the Holy Spirit and 264 in the New Testament. In His dealing with men of all ages, God has used the Holy Spirit to bring about the fulfillment of His divine purposes.

My first book on the Holy Spirit was published in 1968. It was received with a measure of success but has been out of print for more than twenty years. This book is to be an extension and improvement of that first work. I have spent sixty years studying, reflecting, teaching, and preaching on this subject. My hope is that this book will serve as a source of knowledge, comfort, and strength in your goal to live for Christ.

1

CHRISTIANITY 101

BEFORE WE BEGIN our study on the Holy Spirit, there are some basic things essential for us to understand. If we fail, we will not grasp or comprehend the significance of what Christ and the Holy Spirit mean to us as God's people.

God has given us at least five things I would call His gifts to us, an extension of His grace. These five gifts and our understanding of them are basic. The first gift God has given is His Word. We are blessed with Scripture.

The Bible is history, poetry, filled with words of admonition, words of encouragement and comfort, as well as the wisdom and knowledge of God. The Bible is the word of God, and the Holy Spirit plays a very significant role in giving us the Word because it comes to us through Him.

The second gift given to us is the gift of the Son of God Himself who came to earth, lived and died, paying the penalty for our sinfulness. Again, the Holy Spirit is involved in the coming of Jesus. He came upon Jesus at the time of His baptism and was with Him until He left this world.

The third gift He has given us is the gift of the Holy Spirit. The Holy Spirit has been given to us to help us respond in a positive way to the gift of His Son. Romans 8:28 tells us "all things work together for good to those that love God and are called according to His purpose, that you might be transformed into the likeness of his Son." God wants us to be like Jesus. That's our calling, to be like Christ; however, you and I can never successfully do that without divine help. This divine help provided through the Holy Spirit is the primary point of this study, to be examined in later chapters.

The fourth gift He has given us is the church. Sadly, some people say, "I think I can be a good Christian without being associated with the church." This comment indicates a failure to understand the church or its nature. The church is the body of the saved. The church is the family of God. In Ephesians 3:10 "His intent was that now, through the church, the manifold wisdom of God should be made known to the rulers and heavenly realms..." Paul is saying that the church, the very existence of the church, demonstrates the wisdom of God. Unfortunately, some interpret this to mean, "He's saying the church distributes the wisdom of God by preaching the gospel." It's true that the church preaches the gospel, but this is not taught in this verse. The creation of the church is an expression of God's wisdom and is truly a gift to us.

Think of the fellowship we enjoy as God's people, of how we encourage and build each other up and how, together with God's help, we can successfully understand and accomplish the calling, the mission, the purpose He has given us as His people. The church is truly a blessing.

The HS enables and helps us be / transform to be more like Christ.

In 1 Corinthians 6:19, it tells about the body, our bodies being a temple of the Holy Spirit. ("Do you not know that your body is a temple of the Holy Spirit, who is in you, whom you received from God?") Paul also states that the church is the temple of the Holy Spirit, so the Holy Spirit lives within us individually. He also lives within us collectively. Thus, it can be said that the church is the temple of the Holy Spirit, not a building, but us—God's people. The church is a dwelling place of God in the spirit, the Holy Spirit. "Don't you know that you yourselves are God's temple and that God's spirit lives in you?" 1 Corinthians 3:16.

The fifth gift is prayer. Prayer is a gift God gives us. It is the ability to communicate with Him. He communicates with us through the Word; we communicate with Him through prayer. The Holy Spirit plays a role here. The Holy Spirit makes intercession for us, pleading our case before God (Romans 8:26–27), just as Jesus does at the right hand of God right now (Romans 8:34). He's there as an intercessor on our behalf. The Holy Spirit is an intercessor for us. Think about that. The Son of God, seated at the right hand of the Father, pleads our case before the Father. The Holy Spirit, living within us, does the same on our behalf. It is a gift, a blessing. We don't deserve or qualify for this blessing; it is simply another gift of God.

All five things illustrate what is meant by the word *grace*. What we have said in Christianity 101 is that the Bible is a gift of God to man. The coming of the Son of God to make God known and to die on our behalf is a gift. It's an expression of His love, his grace. Thirdly, there is the gift of the Holy Spirit. The church is a gift from God to us. The wisdom of God is obvious to those who understand what the church is. Finally, the magnificent gift of prayer enables us to communicate with the Father, as He so ably communicates with us through His Word and the Holy Spirit.

THE SIN PROBLEM

If I were to give a title to the Bible, it would be "The Sinfulness of Man, the Consequence of Sin, and the Way of Receiving Forgiveness." Everything in Scripture from Genesis to Revelation relates directly or indirectly to man's sin problem. The first component of the sin problem is that we all sin and fall short of the glory of God. We are all sinners, and there is nothing you and I can do to offset the consequences of our sins. Nothing we do can offset that guilt. We are helpless and cannot save ourselves. (Note the apostle Paul's remarks in Romans 1:18–3:23.)

The second part of the sin problem is this: Even though we are Christians and are seeking to follow the Lord, we still sin. God does not want us to sin. He wants us to conduct our lives in a way that reflects Jesus's life. From experience, we know that we are unable to live in a perfect way. As Christians, however, our quest is that we live in a way that reflects the nature of Christ. In 1 John 1:7, the apostle tells us that if we walk in the light (Christ), we have fellowship with God and with each other, and the blood of Christ cleanses us from our sins.

In summary, the first component of the sin problem is to overcome the guilt of sin by receiving forgiveness. The second dilemma is to conduct our lives without sin and to bear the fruit of the Spirit (Galatians 5:22–23). In this way, we honor and glorify our Lord, Jesus Christ.

The solution to first component of the sin problem is found in the gift of Jesus. Many believe that to enter heaven one must simply do more good than evil. Until we understand that doing more good than evil is not the answer, we will never appreciate what Jesus accomplished when He went to the cross. As long as we think we can save ourselves by our own good deeds, it is impossible to grasp the significance of the gift of the Son of God or the gift of the Holy Spirit. If you are saved (forgiven) by our own good deeds, God would be judging on the basis of credits and debits. The theory is, as long as your good deeds outweigh or offset your bad deeds, you stand forgiven before God. The way to Heaven is simply to do more good deeds than bad. In contrast, Paul asked in Galatians 2:21, "I do not set aside the grace of God, for if righteousness could be gained through the law, Christ died for nothing!" If we could save ourselves, why did God send Jesus to the earth? The greatest gift God has ever given man is the gift of His Son. "For God so loved the world that he gave his one and only Son, that whoever believes in him shall not perish but have eternal life" John 3:16.

Apostle Paul writes in Ephesians 2:4-9:

> But because of his great love for us, God, who is rich in mercy, made us alive with Christ even when we were dead in transgressions – it is by grace you have been saved. And God raised us up with Christ and seated us with him in the heavenly realms in Christ Jesus, in order that in the coming ages he might show the incomparable riches of his grace, expressed in his kindness to us in Christ Jesus. For it is by grace you have been saved, through faith – and this not from yourselves, it is the gift of God – not by works, so that no one can boast.

The word *grace* means "gift." If salvation is a gift, it is not deserved. You cannot work for it, you cannot earn it. Jesus is the *gift* God has given us, paying the debt for our sins. Romans 3:24–26 says:

> And we are justified freely by his grace through the redemption that came by Christ Jesus. God presented him as a sacrifice of atonement, through faith in his blood. He did this to demonstrate his justice, because in his forbearance he had left the sins committed beforehand unpunished – he did it to demonstrate his justice at the present time, so as to be just and the one who justifies those who have faith in Jesus.

Since God does not deal with us on the basis of credits and debits, how does he deal with humans and sin then? God deals with man on the basis of law. When you break a law, a penalty must be paid. If you run a corner stoplight, you receive a ticket, a penalty. You decide to contest the penalty before a judge. "Your honor, I did run the red light, but I have stopped at that light countless times. This is the only time I ran it. Do I not receive credit for all the times I stopped at the light?" The judge smiles and assigns the penalty of two hundred dollars for your breaking the law. No credit is given for keeping the law against penalty for future disobedience.

Under God's law, there is no solution to the sin problem, except to pay the penalty: death and separation from God forever. Romans 6:23 says, "For the wages of sin is death, but the gift of God is eternal life in Christ Jesus our Lord." Until you understand this principle, one may never appreciate the cross, the gift of Jesus, the gift of the Holy Spirit, and the gift of the church.

Everything we do in our way of coming to Christ and acknowledging our faith and trust in Him (from our baptism to our worship to our service to our morality) are a response to God's gift, not a qualification for it.

In Romans 3:21 ff, Paul affirms that there is a new righteousness that now comes from God, not by law, but a righteousness that comes through Jesus Christ. He went to the cross and died for our sins and paid the penalty (death) for everyone who has ever lived. In Hebrews 2:9, the author says "He tasted death for everyone." Not every person is going to accept the gift, responding with a life of commitment to Him. This is God's solution for the first component of the sin problem, providing forgiveness for our sins.

The second component of the sin problem is the ability to live our lives bearing the fruit of the Spirit (Galatians 5:22–24: "But the fruit of the Spirit is love, joy, peace, patience, kindness, goodness, faithfulness, gentleness and self-control. Against such things there is no law. Those who belong to Christ Jesus have crucified the sinful nature with its passions and desires") and receive the power to say no to Satan and yes to God. Our success to accomplish this is provided through the indwelling of the Holy Spirit given to all Christians. This is a major point of this study and will be presented in later chapters.

2

IS THE HOLY SPIRIT GOD?

EVIDENCES OF THE
SPIRIT'S PERSONALITY

THE HOLY SPIRIT is a distinct person and is active in all the ways of a personality. The Holy Spirit is not a glorified "it," neither is He a mere influence. He is not an impersonal and vague force, and He is far more than the mind, temper, or disposition of God or Christ. The Holy Spirit is a divine person. He has all the marks of individual personality and is always spoken of, like God and Christ, in the singular number.

The works of the Spirit proclaim His personality. He speaks (1 Timothy 4:11: "Command and teach these things"), He testifies (John 15:26: "When the Counselor comes, whom I will send to you from the Father, the Spirit of truth who goes out from the Father, he will testify about me"), He teaches and reminds the mind (John 14:26), He guides (John 16:12-13), He leads and forbids (Acts 16:6-7: "Paul and his companions traveled throughout the region of Phrygia and Galatia, having been kept by the Holy Spirit from teaching the word in the province of Asia. When they came to the border of Mysia, they tried to enter Bithynia, but the Spirit of Jesus would not allow them to"), He searches (1 Corinthians 2:10: "The Spirit searches all things, even the deep things of God"), He has the characteristics of a person—a mind (Romans 8:27: "And he who searches our hearts knows the mind of the Spirit, because the Spirit intercedes for the saints in accordance with God's will"). (I Corinthians 2:11) "For who among men knows the thoughts of a man except the man's spirit within him? In the same way no one knows the thoughts of God except the Spirit of God."; affection (Romans 15:30) "I urge you, brothers, by our Lord Jesus Christ and by the love of the Spirit, to join me in my struggle by praying to god for me."; will (determines) (I Corinthians 12:11) "All these are the work of one and the same Spirit, and he gives them to each one, just as he determines."; goodness (Nehemiah 9:20 "You gave your good Spirit to instruct them. You did not withhold your manna from their mouths, and you gave them water for their thirst.") He suffers slights and injuries that can only be ascribed to personality. He can be grieved (Ephesians 4:30; Isaiah 63:10) "And do not grieve the Holy Spirit of God, with whom you were sealed for the day of redemption." "Yet they rebelled and grieved his Holy Spirit. So he turned and became their enemy and he himself fought against them." He can be insulted. (Hebrews 10:29 "How much more severely do you think a man deserved to be punished who has trampled the Son of God under foot, who has treated as an unholy thing the blood of the covenant that sanctified him and who has insulted the Spirit of grace?) He can be blasphemed. (Matthew 12:31-32 "And so I tell you, every sin and blasphemy will be forgiven men, but the blasphemy against the Spirit will not be forgiven. Anyone who speaks a word against the Son of man will be forgiven, but anyone who speaks against the Holy Spirit will not be forgiven, either in this age or in the age to come."). He can be resisted (Acts 7:51) "You stiff-necked people, with uncircumcised hearts and ears! You are just like your fathers. You always resist the Holy Spirit." He can be lied unto (Acts 5:3) "Then Peter said, 'Ananias, how is it that Satan has so filled your heart that you have lied to the Holy Spirit and have kept for yourself some of the money you received for the land?". The Spirit has the characteristics of a divine personality. He is eternal (Hebrews 9:14) "How much more, will the blood of Christ, who through the eternal Spirit offered himself unblemished to God, cleanse our consciences from acts that lead to death, so that we may serve the living God!" He is omnipotent. (Ephesians 3:16 "I pray that out of His glorious riches He may strengthen you with power through His Spirit in your inner being.") He is omnipresent. (Psalms 139:7, 10 "Where can I go from your Spirit? Where can I flee from your presence?" "…even there your hand will guide me, your right hand will hold me fast.") His works also manifest divinity: the work of creation (Genesis 1:2; Job 26:13) "Now the earth was formless and empty, darkness was over the surface of the deep, and the Spirit of God was hovering over the waters." "By his breath the skies became fair; his hand pierced the gliding serpent"; the work of regeneration (Titus 3:5) "He saved us, not because of righteous things we had done, but because of His mercy. He saved us through the washing of rebirth and renewal by the Holy Spirit."; the work of resurrecting Jesus and all Christians (Romans 8:11 "And if the Spirit of Him who raised Jesus from the dead is living in you, He who raised Christ from the dead will also give life to your mortal bodies through His Spirit living in you."; He is the source of the miraculous (Matthew 12:28; I Corinthians 12:9,11) "But if I drive out demons by the Spirit of God, then the kingdom of God has come upon you." "...to another faith by the same Spirit, to another gifts of healing by that one Spirit." These attributes and works, which are ascribed to the Holy Spirit, could only belong to a person. Hence, He is, like God and Christ, an individual person. Throughout the Scriptures from beginning to end, we see God, Christ, and the Holy Spirit as divine beings living, speaking, acting, influencing, blessing, reconciling, transforming, loving, and glorifying. The Holy Spirit is thus not seen as a thing but as a glorious person--the Holy Spirit.

THE RELATIONSHIP OF THE SPIRIT TO GOD AND CHRIST

There are three members of the Godhead: God the Father, God the Son, and God the Holy Spirit. In the Old Testament, the Trinity (Triune Godhead) is presented as being composed of God, the originator, author, and supreme ruler of all things; the promised Messiah; and the Holy Spirit, the organizer, life-imparter, law-giver, and guide of the created universe. In the New Testament, they are revealed as the Father, who gave his only begotten Son to save the world; the Son, who became flesh; and the Holy Spirit, who is the Comforter that should abide with the children of God forever and lead them into all truth.

Each member of the Godhead has had his special dispensation with man on the earth. God's dispensation refers to the time beginning with the creation of man to the coming of Christ. During this time, God appeared in different ways and revealed himself in symbols, covenants, various confessions, and teaching. God, through angels and other agencies, spoke to man and instructed him (Hebrews 1:1). At times, God revealed himself and his will to man in visions and dreams. At other times, he spoke through the Holy Spirit to his messengers.

God was prominent and dominant in all the affairs of his people during this dispensation. The dispensation of Christ began when the Word became flesh and dwelt among us, and the Lord began His personal ministry on earth. This doesn't mean, however, that the Father had nothing to do with Christ's dispensation; it simply means that the work of Christ was itself conspicuous, eminent, and salient during this period. This continued until Christ made His ascension back to the Father.

During His personal ministry, Christ walked and talked with men concerning the will of the Father. Following the dispensation of Christ's personal ministry and beginning with the first Pentecost after the resurrection of Christ, the dispensation of the Holy Spirit began. The period of time in which men are now living may be called the Holy Spirit's dispensation. This does not mean that the Holy Spirit had nothing to do during God's dispensation or the dispensation of Christ's personal ministry but that He "now takes the lead" during this age as a member of the Godhead. In fact, all that we know of God and Christ come through the Holy Spirit.

The Bible is entirely a product of the Holy Spirit. In all dispensations, the Holy Spirit is presented as the organizing, life-imparting, law-giving, and guiding personality and representative of the Godhead in the conduct of the material world. But in His dispensation, the Holy Spirit is also particularly active in the spiritual realm. The Holy Spirit is salient and present in all of the work of God and Christ today concerning the redemption of man. He is the executing power of the Godhead during the church age. The Holy Spirit took up the work where Christ left it and carries it on to completion and its final consummation. The Spirit is the ever present helper and guide for the children of the Godhead, dwelling in His temple on earth and, in it, comforting, strengthening and guiding God's people (1 Corinthians 3:16-17).

God promised to abide with them forever. This he was to do in and through the person of the Spirit (John 14:23 "Jesus replied, If anyone loves me, he will obey my teaching. My Father will love him and we will come to him and make our home with him." John 14:16-17 "And I will ask the Father, and he will give you another Counselor to be with you forever- the Spirit of truth. The world cannot accept him, because it neither sees him nor knows him. But you know him, for he lives with you and will be in you." Ephesians 2:22 "And in him you too are being built together to become a dwelling in which God lives by his Spirit.")

Thus, in the order of the unfolding ages, each of the persons of the Godhead in turn exercised an earthly ministry and dealt with man in the work of redemption. These activities are well-summarized by the following statement:

> Under the law, God, the Father, comes down to earth and speaks to men from the cloud of Sinai and from the glory above the mercy seat; under grace, God the Son is in the world, teaching, suffering, dying and rising again; under the dispensation of election and out-gathering now going on the Holy Spirit is here carrying on the work of renewing and sanctifying the church, which is the body of Christ.[1]

In each dispensation, the three members of the Godhead have cooperated, but one member has been more prominently active in each period. At least, one member has been on earth either in person or representatively during each of these dispensations. During each period, the other two members of the Godhead seem in a way to have yielded to the prominence of the one presently represented on earth.

3

The Holy Spirit in the Old Testament

Of the thirty-nine books in the Old Testament, twenty-three refer directly to the Holy Spirit. The same prominence is not given in the Old Testament, to the Holy Spirit that is given in the New Testament. This is probably true because the New Testament deals with the Holy Spirit's dispensation. The Spirit is mentioned in the Old Testament under different names or titles. Sometimes, He is referred to as the Spirit, then as the Spirit of God, Spirit of Jehovah, Spirit of the Lord, and Holy Spirit. Of the eighty-eight distinct references to the Holy Spirit in the Old Testament, there are eighteen different names applied to Him.

THE SPIRIT OF GOD IN RELATION TO GOD

There are no single Old Testament passages that make clear the complete New Testament doctrine of the Trinity and the distinct personality of the Spirit in the full New Testament sense. Such statements as Genesis 1:26 imply a Godhead of more than one person, but a clear distinction between the members of the Godhead is not evident here. There is no clear indication in the Old Testament of a belief that the Spirit of God is a personality distinct from God.

However, there is, as observed in the Old Testament, both an identification of God and the Spirit of God with a distinction between them. The identification is seen in Psalms 139:7 where the omnipresence of the Spirit is declared. "Whither shall I go from thy Spirit? or whither shall I flee from thy presence?" Also, Isaiah 63:10, "But they rebelled and grieved his Holy Spirit" (See also Jeremiah 31:33 and Ezekiel 36:27). In a great number of passages, God and the Spirit of God are not thought of as identical, as in Genesis 1:2, "And the Spirit of God moved upon the face of the waters"; Genesis 6:3, "And Jehovah said, My Spirit shall not strive with man forever"; Psalms 51:11, "And take not thy Holy Spirit from me." (See also Nehemiah 9:20; Psalms 104:29f.) These passages do not prove that God and the Spirit of God were thought of as distinct beings by the Old Testament writers, but only that the Spirit had activities of His own distinct from God. The Spirit was God in action, with a view to accomplishing some particular end or purpose of God. The Spirit was, therefore, God, immanent in man and in the world. Even as an angel of the Lord in certain passages represents both God himself and "one sent" by God, so in like manner the Spirit of God was both God within or upon man and at the same time one sent by

God to man. There are several Old Testament passages that are in harmony with the Trinitarian concept of the New Testament; Isaiah 48:16, "And now the Lord Jehovah hath sent me and his Spirit. " Also, Haggai 2: 5, "And my Spirit abode among you" (See also Zechariah 4:6; Psalms 51: 11; Genesis 1:2; Nehemiah 9:20; Psalms 104:29f.)

THE SPIRIT IN NATURE

Old Testament writers regarded the phenomena of nature as the result of God's direct action through his Spirit. The manifestations of the Holy Spirit in the Old Testament begin with the dawn of creation. The Holy Spirit first appeared in the creation, "And the Spirit of God moved upon the face of the waters" (Genesis 1:2). Here the Holy Spirit brings order and beauty out of the primeval chaos and conducts the cosmic forces toward the goal of an ordered universe. In Job 26:13, the beauty of the heavens is ascribed to the Spirit: "By his Spirit the heavens are garnished." So here He is, the wonder worker in the material universe. This same thought is expressed in Psalms 104:28-30, "Thou send forth thy Spirit, they are created; and thou renew the face of the ground." (See also Isaiah 32: 15; Job 32:8; 33:4; Psalms 33:6.)

THE SPIRIT OF GOD IN MAN

The Spirit was thought of as imparting natural powers, both physical and intellectual, to man. Also, the extraordinary powers exhibited by the Israelites on occasion were usually attributed to the Spirit. It is noted that such gifts and powers, conferred by the Holy Spirit for service in God's kingdom, were upon men who already had a degree of power, wisdom, or knowledge in performing certain skills. The Holy Spirit thus heightened their ability and power.

Normal powers. In Genesis 2:7 God originates man's personal and intellectual life by breathing into his nostrils "the breath of life." Physical life is declared to be due to the presence of the Spirit of God (Job 27:3). Elihu, in Job 33:4, says, "The Spirit of God has made me, and the breath of the Almighty gives me life." Man is, thus, regarded by the Old Testament writers in all parts of his being, body, mind, and spirit as the direct result of the action of the Spirit of God.

Extraordinary powers. The greater part of the Old Testament passages, which refer to the Spirit of God in man, have to do with gifts and powers conferred by the Holy Spirit for unusual service in the furthering of the kingdom of God. The Holy Spirit seems to have guided men in their ability to work for Jehovah, "And I have filled him with the Spirit of God in wisdom and in understanding and in knowledge and in all manner of workmanship" (Exodus 31:3). Here God heightened the ability and skill of Bezalel. In the book of Judges 3:10, the Holy Spirit conferred powers upon the judges and warriors. "The Spirit of God came upon Othniel and he judged Israel." God heightened his ability and power. In Judges 6:34, the Spirit came upon Gideon, and, in Judges 11: 29, He came upon Jephthah. In Judges 14:6, the Spirit of God came mightily upon Samson, and he was able to kill a lion. These demonstrations of the Spirit's power in the Old Testament make it apparent that they were for the purpose of imparting great strength and valor to God's chosen commanders who were to lead his people to victory against their foes. It may be noted that the Spirit imparted these special endowments of power without reference to the moral character of the recipient.

Other Old Testament characters who received extraordinary powers through the Holy Spirit include Daniel, who is represented as having wisdom to interpret dreams through the Spirit and, afterwards because of the Spirit, was exalted to a position of authority and power (Daniel 4:8; 5:11-14; 6:3). Joseph was also able to interpret the Pharaoh's dream through the Spirit of God (Genesis 41:16, 38). In Nehemiah 9:20, it is stated that the Spirit was given to the people for instruction and strengthening during the wilderness wanderings and to the elders, along with Moses (Numbers 11:17, 25). The Holy Spirit is mentioned in connection with the construction of the temple (1 Chronicles 28:11-12) and in the rebuilding of the temple (Zechariah 4:6-7). These activities of the Spirit reflected in the life of the people.

THE SPIRIT IN OLD TESTAMENT PROPHECY

A most distinctive and important manifestation of the Spirit's activity in the Old Testament was in the sphere of prophecy. The word *prophet* means "one who speaks for God." When God had a new message for his people or when he wanted to press the old message on their consciences, he sent the Spirit, not upon the multitude but upon a chosen messenger or messengers. The Spirit then was able to move the mind of the multitude through the mind, voice, and life of the prophetic messenger. The extent to which the ordinary individual being taught received the Spirit was the extent to which he willingly accepted the truth through God's inspired messenger.

Thus, the prophet was God's mouthpiece to the people, being distinguished from others as the man who possessed the Spirit of God (Hosea 9:7). These men of God were not chiefly concerned about future events but were pre-eminently and conspicuously reformers and teachers of the law. They did not ordinarily only begin their messages with the phrase, "Thus says Jehovah," or its equivalent, but they also ascribed their messages directly to the Spirit of God (Ezekiel 2:2; 8:3; 11:1, 24). Many of the prophets declared that they were speaking by the Holy Spirit. Isaiah said, "The Spirit of the Lord Jehovah is upon me" (Isaiah 61:1). And Jeremiah said, "Now the word of Jehovah came unto me" (Jeremiah 1:4). Ezekiel said, "The Spirit lifted me up and brought me unto the east gate of Jehovah's house" (Ezekiel 11:1 and 11:5). In Nehemiah 9:30 the prophets were said to have spoken by the Spirit, "Yet many years did you bear with them, and testified against them by thy Spirit through thy prophets." David also spoke by the Holy Spirit, "The Spirit of Jehovah spoke by me, and his word was upon my tongue" (2 Samuel 23:2). The New Testament honors the Old Testament as being the words of the Holy Spirit. Peter said, "For no prophecy ever came by the will of man: but men spoke from God, being moved by the Holy Spirit" (2 Peter 1:21; cf I Peter 1:9-10). "All the major prophets claimed the Holy Spirit for what they said." The Old Testament clearly and frequently emphasizes the fact that the Holy Spirit appeared in God's revelation to man.

The Old Testament prophets also gave good evidence for the hope that in the last days the Spirit would be given to all of God's people (Ezekiel 36:27 "And I will put my Spirit in you and move you to follow my decrees and be careful to keep my laws."; Ezekiel 37:14; 39:29; Isaiah 44:3;

Joel 2:28 "And afterward, I will pour out my Spirit on all people. Your sons and daughters will prophesy, your old men will dream dreams, your young men will see visions." Zechariah 12:10). There is no doubt that the early church thought that these prophecies were fulfilled in its time.

THE SPIRIT IN THE MESSIAH

In the book of Isaiah, there are several distinct references to the Spirit in connection with the Messiah. The Messiah is conceived as the ideal king, who springs from the root of David in some instances and in others as the suffering Servant of Jehovah (Isaiah 53). In Isaiah 11:15, a picture of the "shoot out of the stock of Jesse" is given. The Spirit imparts wisdom and understanding and endows him with manifold gifts. In Isaiah 42:1, the "servant" is, in like manner, endowed with gifts of the Spirit by virtue of which he shall bring forth justice to the Gentiles. In Isaiah 61:1ff occur the words which Jesus quotes and applies to himself in Luke 4:12ff, beginning, "The Spirit of the Lord is upon me…" In these passages, the prophet Isaiah describes the Messiah as having a wide range of powers, all of which can be traced to the action of God's Spirit.

4

THE HOLY SPIRIT IN THE NEW TESTAMENT—THE GOSPELS

THE NEW TESTAMENT presents a wide range of activities of the Holy Spirit; His person, advent, work, and relation to Christ are all discussed in the New Testament. There are about 264 references to the Holy Spirit in the New Testament. The following names are found in New Testament passages for the Holy Spirit: the Spirit (Romans 8:13); Spirit of God (Romans 8:14); Spirit of Christ (Romans 8:9); Spirit himself (Romans 8:16); Spirit of God's Son (Galatians 4:6); Spirit of the Father (Matthew 10:20); Spirit of truth (John 14:15-17); Holy Spirit (Acts 28:25); Comforter (John 14:26).

The dispensation of the Spirit is clearly seen in the New Testament, and, for this reason, the New Testament may well be called "The Book of the Holy Spirit." The Old Testament writers were aware of the Spirit's action upon inanimate nature, and they attributed any unusual manifestation of power of a human spirit to an intervention of the Spirit of God. The New Testament writers, however, made it evident that the Holy Spirit was not only the channel for abnormal manifestations of spiritual power but that in New Testament times and during the age of the church, it would also remain with man as an abiding source of life and the agent of righteousness.

In the Birth and Ministry of John the Baptist

John the Baptist is the first reformer whose name appears in the New Testament. John was a great prophet, but he was also a great reformer with the power of God in and back of him. In his case, as with the ancient prophets, God sent his Spirit on to the preacher and through him into the message and through it into the hearts and lives of the people. Prior to John the Baptist's birth, an angel appeared unto his father, Zacharias, and foretold that his wife would bear a son who would do great things. The angel also said concerning John, "And he shall be filled with the Holy Spirit even from his mother's womb" (Luke 1:13-17). In connection with John's birth, his mother, Elizabeth, and Zacharias were filled with the Holy Spirit sufficiently to have supernatural knowledge of things, and even to utter prophecy (Luke 1:41ff and 1:67ff).

Although John was a Spirit-inspired prophet bringing God's message to the people, he was a non-literary prophet, for he did not leave any writings. During his ministry, John testified to the Holy Spirit descending upon Christ at his baptism (John 1:32, 33) and taught that though he baptized the disciples with water, Jesus would baptize them with the Holy Spirit (Matthew 3:11).

IN THE LIFE AND MINISTRY OF JESUS

The Holy Spirit was active in the birth of Jesus. In Luke 1:30ff, an angel appears unto Mary and tells her that she shall bear a son and calls attention to the high position that Jesus will hold. He, thus, tells Mary (v. 35) that this miracle will occur when the Holy Spirit comes upon her. This passage and Matthew 1:18, 20 set forth the supernatural origin of Jesus's earthly life.

Not only was the Holy Spirit prominent in the incarnation, but He also accompanied the Lord. Great emphasis is given in particular to the descent of the Spirit upon Jesus at his baptism, "and straightway coming up out of the water he saw the heavens rent asunder and the Spirit as a dove descending upon him" (Mark 1:8-10; cf Luke 3:16-22; Matthew 3:11-16). The baptism of Jesus and this reception of the Holy Spirit brought to a close his private life and introduced him to his public ministry.

Soon after his baptism, Christ was led by the Holy Spirit into the wilderness where he endured the temptations (Matthew 4:1-11; Luke 4:1, 14). The Holy Spirit continued His presence, influence, and cooperation with Christ during all his personal ministry. It was prophesied that the Holy Spirit would be with the Messiah, and the fulfillment of this prophecy was claimed by Christ in Matthew 12:18 and Luke 4:18ff. God gave the Holy Spirit in His fullness, "without measure" to Christ as the Messiah (John 3:34).

Jesus worked signs and miracles through the power of the Spirit (Acts 10:38 "We are witnesses of everything he did in the country of the Jews and in Jerusalem. They killed him by hanging him on a tree"). In Matthew 12:28 ("But if I drive out demons by the Spirit of God, then the kingdom of God has come upon you.") and Luke 11:20, Christ is said to have cast out devils by the Spirit of God. The signs and miracles that Christ did were evidences of the Holy Spirit in him. It is clear that the New Testament writers thought of the entire public life of Christ as aided by the Spirit of God.

The Holy Spirit was also with Christ at his death and resurrection. In Hebrews 9:14, it is declared that Christ "through the eternal Spirit offered himself without blemish unto God." Romans 8:11 ("And if the Spirit of him who raised Jesus from the dead is living in you, he who raised Christ from the dead will also give life to your mortal bodies through his Spirit, who lives in you") states that Christ was raised from the dead by the Holy Spirit.

The Holy Spirit was with Christ at birth. Throughout his earthly life, he was filled with the Spirit's power and influence. The Holy Spirit was with him in his ministry, his death, his resurrection and ascension.

THE TEACHINGS OF JESUS ON THE HOLY SPIRIT

In the Synoptic Gospels, Jesus taught that the Spirit of the Lord was upon him and this was a fulfillment of Isaiah 61:1ff (Luke 4:16ff). He taught that the Father would give the Holy Spirit to those who asked for Him, "If ye then being evil, know how to give good gifts unto your children, how much more shall your heavenly Father give the Holy Spirit to them that ask him?" (Luke 11:13). Jesus recognized the Holy Spirit as a source of inspiration for the Scriptures (Matthew 22:43 "He said to them, How is it then that David, speaking by the Spirit, calls him Lord?"); Matthew 10:20; Luke 12:12; Mark 13:11). The Lord promised the Spirit to the apostles and declared that He would guide them as to what they should say. This promise is fulfilled in Acts 2 and Acts 4:8-12.

In Matthew 12:31 ("And so I tell you, every sin and blasphemy will be forgiven men, but the blasphemy against the Spirit will not be forgiven."); Mark 3:28-29 "I tell you the truth, all the sins and blasphemies of men will be forgiven them. But whoever blasphemes against the Holy Spirit will never be forgiven; he is guilty of an eternal sin." In Luke 12:10, there is the declaration by Christ that blasphemy against the Holy Spirit is an unpardonable sin. The charge made against Christ in the passages mentioned was that he cast out devils by Beelzebub, the prince of devils. It is evident that the blasphemy against the Spirit was not only a rejection of Jesus and his works but was also the sin of ascribing works of divine nature and power, which had all the marks of their origin in the goodness of God, to a diabolic source such as Satan.

The unpardonable sin mentioned here by our Lord has been interpreted by some to refer to a sin for which no repentance has been made. While it is certainly true that God will not forgive our sins unless we have a penitent attitude, there is no evidence that, in the context of the passages where the unpardonable sin is mentioned, this is a correct interpretation. On the other hand, the context seems to make it quite clear that the sin against the Holy

Spirit, referred to as the unpardonable sin or blasphemy against the Holy Spirit, is a sin that credits the works of God's Spirit as being the works of Satan. A parallel situation today might be the man who would advocate that the Bible is the work of Satan rather than of God or his Spirit.

The Lord's final teaching on the Holy Spirit in the Gospels is found in the Great Commission. Christ commanded the disciples to baptize in the name of the Father, the Son, and the Holy Spirit (Matthew 28:19 "Therefore go and make disciples of all nations, baptizing them in the name of the Father and of the Son and of the Holy Spirit").

In the Gospel of John, which is the fourth gospel, there is a more elaborate presentation of the office and work of the Holy Spirit, particularly in chapters 14-16. In John 3:3-5, Jesus declares the activity of the Spirit in the new birth, "Except one be born of the water and the Spirit, he cannot enter into the kingdom of heaven." In John 7:39, "By this he meant the Spirit, whom those who believed in him were later to receive. Up to that time the Spirit had not been given, since Jesus had not yet been glorified." The Spirit is promised by Christ to those who would believe in him. The Holy Spirit was not given to believers until after Christ's death and ascension (Acts 2:38: "Peter replies, Repent and be baptized, every one of you, in the name of Jesus Christ for the forgiveness of your sins. And you will receive the gift of the Holy Spirit").

In chapters 14-16, John records the Lord's last discourse to his disciples before his death. In this passage, there is some of the most extensive teaching by Christ on the Holy Spirit. The Holy Spirit is promised to the apostles by Christ, "and I will pray the Father, and he shall give you another Comforter, that he may be with you forever, even the Spirit of truth" (John 14:16; cf. John 14:26). The Lord declares that the Holy Spirit will come from the Father and that one of His principal works will be to testify of Christ (John 15:26 "When the Counselor of truth comes, whom I will send to you from the Father, the Spirit of truth who goes out from the Father, he will testify about me").

In John 16:7-15, Jesus taught that the Holy Spirit could not come until after Jesus had returned to his Father. When the Holy Spirit came, He would convict the world of sin, righteousness, and judgment. The Holy Spirit was not to bring an absolutely new teaching, but He would bring to the minds of the apostles all the words that Jesus had spoken and would add those things, which were now in the mind of Christ and at the present time he was keeping from the apostles as they were not able to understand them. In verse 15, Jesus claims all the teachings of the Spirit as his.

The teachings in John 14-16 on the Holy Spirit may be summed up as follows: He is the Spirit of truth; He guides into all truth; He brings into memory Christ's teaching; He shows things to come; He glorifies Christ; He speaks not of himself but of Christ; He, like believers, bears witness to Christ, He enables the apostles to do greater works than those of Christ; He convicts the world of sin, of righteousness, and judgment; He comes because Christ goes away; He is another Comforter; and He is to abide with the disciples forever.

5

THE HOLY SPIRIT IN THE NEW TESTAMENT—IN THE CHURCH

A CLEARER AND more concise understanding of the Holy Spirit in the rest of the New Testament may be obtained by studying the various works of the Spirit after Pentecost (Acts 2). The New Testament Scriptures speak of the Holy Spirit in connection with God's revelation to man (John 16:13), of the baptism of the Holy Spirit (Matthew 3:11 "I baptize you with water for repentance But after me will come one who is more powerful than I, whose sandals I am not fit to carry. He will baptize you with the Holy Spirit and with fire"), of the gifts of the Spirit (1 Corinthians 12), of the work of the Spirit in conversion (Titus 3:4-7), and of the reception of the Spirit by the children of God (Romans 8:15).

IN THE INSPIRATION OF THE MAN OF GOD AND OF THE SCRIPTURES

As previously noted, the Old Testament frequently emphasizes the fact that the Holy Spirit appeared in God's revelation to man (2 Samuel 23:1-2; Isaiah 61:1; Jeremiah 1:4;
Ezekiel 11:1, 5; etc.). The New Testament also emphasizes
that the Holy Spirit was active in inspiring men of God in
oral expressions and in written truth. Jesus promised his
apostles that he would send them the Holy Spirit, who
would guide them into all truth, teach them all things, bring
all that he had taught them to remembrance, and foretell
things to come (John 14-16). In Luke 12:11–12, the Lord
exhorted the apostles to not worry about what they should
say: "For the Holy Spirit shall teach you in that very hour
what ye ought to say."

The apostle Paul declared that he spoke "not in words
which man's wisdom teaches, but which the Spirit teaches"
(I Corinthians 2:10-13). Also, in 1 Timothy 4:1, Paul begins
a section with the phrase, "But the Spirit says expressly…"
In 2 Timothy 3:16, it says, "All scripture is God-breathed
and is useful for teaching, rebuking, correcting, and training
in righteousness." Paul declares that all scripture is inspired
of God. However, the Spirit is not specifically mentioned
in this verse.

Although the apostle Peter makes no reference to the
inspiration of New Testament writers, he states that the
Holy Spirit spoke through the Old Testament prophets.
"For no prophecy ever came by the will of man; but men
spoke from God being moved by the Holy Spirit" (II Peter
1:19-21; cf. I Peter 1: 10–11).

Man is dependent upon the word in order to know
God's divine will. That God has chosen to reveal himself

to man is truly an expression of his great love for us. God's love and mercy and his divine will are all made known to us through his Spirit: "The things of God none knows, save the Spirit of God" (1 Corinthians 2:11).

THE HOLY SPIRIT'S ACTIVITY IN ACTS 2 AND 10

John the Baptist predicted that Jesus would baptize by the Holy Spirit ((Matthew 3:11; Mark 1:8; Luke 3:16). We have already noted in the Old Testament that prophecies were made regarding the Holy Spirit under the New Covenant (Ezekiel 44:5; Joel 2:28; Zechariah 12:10).

The expression "baptized by the Spirit" is found only in the above New Testament passages as well as 1 Corinthians 12:13. At one time, I believed this expression referred only to the coming of the Holy Spirit's power on the apostles in Acts 2:1–4 and on Cornelius and his household in Acts 10:44–48. However, in 1 Corinthians 12:13, Paul says, "We were all baptized by one Spirit into one body," and in John 3:5 and Titus 3:5, baptism is connected to receiving the Holy Spirit. These latter verses caused me to question my former conclusion. I now believe that the expression "baptized by the Holy Spirit" is a general reference to include all the Holy Spirit's activity in the early church as well as in the church today. The word *baptism* is a Greek word. When *baptism* is translated into English, the word would be *immersion*. Therefore, to be baptized by the Spirit means immersed into the Spirit, overwhelmed by the Spirit, filled with the Spirit.

The assertion that Jesus would baptize with the Holy Spirit would include: Acts 2:1–4 (apostles, a fulfillment of

John 14–16, and Joel 2:28), Acts 10:44–8 (Cornelius, the first Gentile Christian), Acts 2:38, 5:32, 1 John 3:5, Titus 3:5 (all baptized believers), Acts 8:4–8, 1, and Corinthians 12:7–11 (selected early Christians given the gift of prophecy and other miraculous gifts).

The purpose of the Holy Spirit coming upon the apostles (Acts 2:1–4) seems to have been twofold. One purpose was that it enabled them to bear witness for Christ. They were ready to preach the gospel to the whole creation, but they first needed the Holy Spirit to guide them into all truth. Christ had promised them the Spirit for this very purpose (John 16:7–15). A second purpose was that they received the ability to speak with tongues (foreign languages), which became a sign to those who heard that they were men of God. The apostles used their miraculous powers to convince the people that what they spoke was truly the Word of God. (Mark 16:1, Acts 2:43, Hebrews 2:4).

The special reason for the Holy Spirit coming into Cornelius's household was also for a sign. The ability of these Gentiles to speak with other tongues became a sign to Peter and other Jewish brethren that God would also accept Gentiles into his kingdom. By seeing the Gentiles receive the Holy Spirit, even as did the apostles on Pentecost, the Jews could perceive that God is truly no respecter of persons (Acts 10:34). Notice that the Spirit coming on to Cornelius and his household was the only time this manifestation of the Spirit was given anyone prior to their becoming a Christian. With the extreme prejudice the Jews held against the Gentiles, such a miracle was necessary to convince the Jewish Christians that God would accept Gentiles into the church.

SPIRITUAL GIFTS

In the period of the early church, God gave to some of his adopted children various miraculous powers referred to by Paul as gifts of the Holy Spirit. In 1 Corinthians 12:4–11, Paul names the nine distinct spiritual gifts, all of which involve miraculous powers.

> There are different kinds of gifts, but the same Spirit. There are different kinds of service, but the same Lord. There are different kinds of working, but the same God works all of them in all men. Now to each one the manifestation of the Spirit is given for the common good. To one there is given through the Spirit the message of wisdom, to another the message of knowledge by means of the same Spirit, to another faith by the same Spirit, to another gifts of healing by that one Spirit, to another miraculous powers, to another prophecy, to another distinguishing between spirits, to another speaking in different kinds of tongue, and to still another the interpretation of tongues. All these are the work of one and the same Spirit, and he gives them to each one, just as he determines.

These gifts were to be used by those Christians who possessed them for the general edification of the church, not for their own self-glorification. The chief end of the use of all these gifts was "that the church might receive instruction" (1 Corinthians 14:6). In this connection, spiritual gifts were given to help confirm the preaching of the Word, that all who heard the gospel might know that the one who spoke was from God (Mark 16:20; Hebrews 2:1–4). They were to help with the revelation from God until the New Testament was completed. (1 Corinthians 13:9–12).

This manifestation of "gifts" of the Spirit was also an endowment of the miraculous. The ability to perform these miraculous acts by the Holy Spirit was obtained through the laying on of apostolic hands and prayer. That the apostles were the only men to bestow these spiritual gifts is seen from the following passages. In Acts 6:6, the apostles laid their hands upon the first deacons of the church, including Philip and Stephen. They were able to perform signs and wonders. (Acts 6:8; 8:6) Then in Acts 8:12, Philip performed miracles and preached the gospel, and many Samaritans believed and were baptized. It was necessary for Peter and John to come from Jerusalem to give the Samaritans the power of spiritual gifts, showing that Philip, although able to perform miracles, did not have the power to bestow such gifts. In Romans 1:11, Paul, an apostle, told the Romans that he desired to give them a spiritual gift. Timothy had received a gift by the hands of the apostle Paul (2 Timothy 1:6). In all cases where spiritual gifts were given, an apostle was instrumental in conferring them.

In Conversion

That the Holy Spirit is active in the conversion of alien sinners is evident from many passages of Scripture. "Except a man be born of the water and of the Spirit he cannot enter into the kingdom of heaven" (John 3:5). Again, "And He, (the Holy Spirit) when He is come, will convict the world in respect of sin, and of righteousness and of judgment" (John 16:8). And, "According to his mercy he saved us, by the washing of regeneration and the renewing of the Holy Spirit" (Titus 3:4-7). These and other New Testament passages clearly show that the Holy Spirit is active in conversion. But how does the Holy Spirit operate on the minds and hearts of the people in order to bring them into Christ?

The apostles were placed in charge of the work of converting the world to Christ, and they were to do it by preaching (Mark 16:15-16). The Holy Spirit was sent to the apostles to endow them for their work and to guide them unto all truth. The Spirit was received by the apostles on the day of Pentecost (Acts 2), and there, through the words of Peter, the Spirit reproved the world. The multitude understood and many believed, being moved by the Holy Spirit through the words of the apostle. When we hear the words of an inspired man of God, we hear the words of the Spirit, and when we have the thoughts legitimately belonging to such words, we have the thoughts communicated by the Spirit. The Spirit and the Word work together harmoniously. There is no evidence that in conversion they ever worked apart. Thus, the Holy Spirit uses the Word as the instrument through which He operates on the minds and hearts of alien sinners.

That the Holy Spirit operates in conversion only through the instrumentality of the Word is seen from a close study of the following New Testament passages: "For I am not ashamed of the gospel of Christ for it is the power of God unto salvation to everyone that believeth" (Romans 1:16). James 1:21 also says, "Wherefore putting away all filthiness and overflowing of wickedness, receive with meekness the implanted word, which is able to save your souls." It is by faith that God purifies the heart (Acts 15:9), and yet faith comes by hearing the Word of God (Romans 10:17). In 1 Corinthians 4:14–15, it states, "For in Christ Jesus I have begotten you through the gospel." The Spirit is the author of the gospel. Ephesians 6:17 says, "And take the helmet of salvation, and the sword of the Spirit, which is the word of God." In 1 Peter 1:23, it also says, "Having been begotten again, not of corruptible seed, but of incorruptible, through the word of God which lives and abides." John 8:32 states, "You shall know the truth and the truth shall make you free." The narrative of Stephen in Acts 7 shows clearly that the Spirit was located in Stephen and through his words operated on the people; yet they did not receive the Spirit but resisted it instead. Persons operated on by the Spirit through the Word may receive or reject its teaching, as they choose. In all the examples of conversion mentioned in the New Testament, the Gospel as God's power to save is heard, believed, and obeyed.

From these Scriptures, it is evident that the Holy Spirit operates upon the heart of the sinner in conversion through the truth, and that truth is the Gospel message, the Word of God. The New Testament does not teach that the Holy Spirit operates in any other way in conversion than through the instrumentality of the Word.

While it is the message that opens our hearts to Christ, once we respond to that message in obedience to the Gospel (1 Thessalonians 1:8), we are united with the Holy Spirit. When we are buried with Christ in baptism, (Romans 6:3–4 and Galatians 3:27), we receive both the remission of our sins (having been cleansed by the blood of Jesus) and the gift of the Holy Spirit (Acts 2:38).

Both Jesus and Paul comment on our being united with Christ the moment we receive the Holy Spirit. Jesus says we are born of the Spirit and of the water in John 3:5. Paul says we are saved through the washing of rebirth and renewal by the Spirit (Titus 3:5). Receiving the Spirit is the beginning of our spiritual lives. We are now new creatures with a new Spirit living within us. We have been born again, resurrected from a life of sin, made alive in Christ (Romans 8:11). The apostle Paul states we have been baptized by one Spirit into one body (the church). "For we were all baptized by one Spirit into one body—whether Jews or Greeks, slave or free—and we were all given the one Spirit to drink" (1 Corinthians 12:13).

Refer to Chapter 9 for a more thorough discussion of the reception of the Holy Spirit by the Christian.

IN THE PERSONAL LIFE OF THE CHRISTIAN

It is this phase of the Holy Spirit's work that the next eight chapters will discuss. It will suffice here to point out that the New Testament teaches that the Holy Spirit "dwells in" the faithful Christian. "Know you not that your body is a temple of the Holy Spirit which is in you, which you have from God?" (I Corinthians 6:19). The Spirit is given by God to those who obey him (Acts 5:32).

The indwelling of the Spirit differs from spiritual gifts in that it is void of the miraculous, and, in this sense, it is similar to the Holy Spirit's work in conversion. While the Holy Spirit dwelt in the apostles and many of the early Christians in an extraordinary sense, He dwells as an abiding gift in the mind, heart, and conscience of every obedient believer. The Holy Spirit enables the Christian to bring forth abundantly in his life the fruit of the Spirit (Galatians 5:22–23). He strengthens him with might, even in the inner man (Ephesians 3:16), and He helps his weaknesses and makes intercession for him (Romans 8:26-27).

Henry B. Swete gives the following summary of the Spirit's activities as presented in God's Word:

> The Spirit appears first in connection with the cosmogony of Genesis, and the writers of the Old Testament frequently refer to His work in sustaining and renewing physical life. But the Hebrew Canon attributes to Him also the endowment of human nature with intellectual and spiritual gifts, and especially regard Him as the source of the great gift of prophecy. It speaks of Him as the author of moral purity and religious consecration. Lastly, it foretells the coming of an ideal king, a perfect Servant of God, in whom the Spirit should rest in his fullness, and an extension of the Spirit's gifts in the last days to the whole nation and to the world. At this point the New Testament takes up the thread of the revelation. The Synoptic Gospels show how the ideals of the Old Testament were fulfilled in the life and ministry of Jesus Christ. The fourth Gospel predicts the mission of the Spirit to the Church; the Acts and Epistles relate the fulfillment of His mission in the experience of the Apostolic Church. We are permitted to see how it has changed the whole spiritual order, raising a new Israel out of the old, transforming an elect nation into a catholic church, pouring new life into the body of the disciples, sanctifying individual wills, carrying conviction to the world and guiding believers into the fullness of truth. In St. Paul's writings the biblical doctrine of the operations of the Holy Spirit reaches its completion. The apostle sees in the Spirit of Christ the source of the vital unity which inspires the Church, the quickening and compacting power of the new creation. But he teaches with equal clearness that

the Spirit has come to regenerate and restore the personal life of each of the baptized, dwelling in the body as His temple, identifying Himself with the human spirit in its struggle with the flesh and its striving after God, until He has perfected the nature which the Son of God redeemed and has raised it to the measure of the stature of the fullness of Christ.[1]

6

THE WORK OF THE HOLY SPIRIT IN THE LIFE OF THE CHRISTIAN—HIS PURPOSE

THE HOLY SPIRIT is active in the Christian's life. His work does not cease with man's conversion to Christ, but He abides in the Christian and works in him and for him to bring about his ultimate redemption. The works of the Holy Spirit in relation to the Christian are many. It is by the Holy Spirit that he is sanctified. The Spirit instructs, guides, comforts, and consoles the Christian. The Spirit bears witness with his spirit that he is a child of God. He enables the Christian to bring forth the fruit of the Spirit in his life. The Spirit helps him in his infirmities and makes intercession for him. The Holy Spirit strengthens the inner man and helps him to overcome sin and resist the flesh. The Christian is made free and kept free by the Spirit of God. He is the source of joy, hope, and love in the Christian life. God has not left the Christian alone to "fight the good fight of faith." Man can be assured that he has God's help through the Holy Spirit in his every effort to follow after the Lord and Savior, Jesus Christ.

Part of the Holy Spirit's work in the life of the Christian is done through the instrumentality of the written Word. The remainder of His work He accomplishes as He dwells in the heart of the faithful Christian, where He abides in fulfillment of God's promise to those who have obeyed him.

THE PURPOSE OF THE SPIRIT'S WORK

The Holy Spirit plays an important part in the life of the Christian. God has blessed the Christian with the written Word and with the "gift of the Holy Spirit" for a specific purpose. It is through these means that the child of God is instructed and aided by the Holy Spirit in living a life that will lead to his eternal salvation. It is the work of the Holy Spirit to carry forward progressively the work of God in the human soul, until it is transformed into the likeness of Christ. Man, in all his weaknesses and moral imperfections, is led by the Spirit to a unity, completeness, and fullness of life and love. This process, which begins with man's spiritual birth and is carried on until he is transformed into the image of Christ (Romans 8:29), is called sanctification. It is the primary work of the Holy Spirit in the life of the Christian.

Sanctification

To sanctify means to set apart or to make holy. "This may be done in a moment and, so far as a mere state or relation is concerned, it is as instantaneous as baptism."[1] "But there is a holy character, as well as a holy state, and in the formation of a holy character, sanctification is unquestionably a progressive work."[2] In the latter sense, sanctification includes the growth and development involved in becoming holy.

The English word *sanctification* comes from two Latin words, "sanctus," which means "holy," and "facio," which means "to make." Thus, sanctification is the process of becoming holy or separate. It is a progressive work begun in the conversion of the sinner and carried on in the life of the Christian unto perfection. Although it is impossible to reach the high hope and great goal of perfection in the flesh, the Christian works toward that end in order that he may attain perfection in glory. The New Testament teaches that the whole Christian life is to be one process of sanctification. Sanctification may be distinguished from conversion as growth is distinguished from birth. It is the perfecting of the saint, the bringing of the newborn babe up into the measure of the stature of the fullness of Christ. It is the putting off the "old man" and putting on the "new man." (Note Ephesians 4:22-24: "You were taught, with regard to your former way of life, to put off your old self, which is being corrupted by its deceitful desires; to be made new in the attitude of your minds; and to put on the new self, created to be like God in true righteousness and holiness.") The babe in Christ is a new creature; old things have passed away, and all things have become new. Now that he is in the family of God, he must adjust to the new surroundings in the spiritual kingdom and must grow and develop as a child of God. This growth and development, which is called sanctification, is a work of the Holy Spirit, which enables believers in Christ more and more to die to sin and live unto righteousness. Having been adopted into the family of God, Christian men and women are led by the Spirit of God in growth and development in the Christian life.

The characteristic name of the Spirit in the New Testament is "Holy," meaning separate or apart. The primary work of the Spirit in the life of the Christian is to make him holy or set him apart: to sanctify him.

Note the following Scriptures:

> But we are bound to give thanks to God always for you, brethren, beloved of the Lord, for that God chose you from the beginning unto salvation in sanctification of the Spirit and belief of the truth.
>
> 2 Thessalonians 2:13

> And such were some of you: but ye were washed, but ye were sanctified, but ye were justified in the name of the Lord Jesus Christ, and in the Spirit of our God.
>
> 1 Corinthians 6:11

> That I should be a minister of Christ Jesus unto the Gentiles, ministering the gospel of God, that the offering up of the Gentiles might be made acceptable, being sanctified by the Holy Spirit.
>
> Romans 15:16

The ultimate aim of all the Spirit's work is to develop and perfect the Christian into the likeness of Christ. In a sense, all of the Spirit's work is included in the process of sanctification. All that the Spirit does Himself and through the instrumentality of the written Word is looking toward the sanctification of the Christian until he attains a perfect holiness of character in the life to come.

God, through the Holy Spirit, sanctifies as much of man's life as is yielded to him. He fills as much of the human heart as is opened to him. So Christian growth consists of this—that as more and more of the heart is opened to God, the more the Christian can be sanctified. Sanctification cannot be forced upon an unyielding Christian.

Although it is the duty and work of the Christian to perfect holiness in the fear of the Lord, it requires God's aid received through the Holy Spirit.

> While the Commands, believe, repent and be baptized are never accompanied with any intimation of peculiar difficulty; the commands to the use of the means of spiritual health and life; to form the Christian character; to attain the resurrection of the just; to lay hold on eternal life; to make our calling and election sure, are accompanied with such exhortations, admonitions, cautions, as to make it a difficult and critical affair, requiring all the aid of the Spirit of our God, to all the means of grace and untiring diligence and perseverance on our part."[3]

The Holy Spirit actually and powerfully assists the Christian. The Spirit is the author of man's holiness and is in the struggle to live victoriously over sin and temptation. He works in and with the Christian to bring about his sanctification.

THE FRUIT OF THE SPIRIT

The result of the work of sanctification is called the fruit of the Spirit (Galatians 5:22ff). Sanctification is growth, and the holy life is fruit. When the Spirit leads a man, there is movement and progress in his life as step after step he follows the Spirit's influence, each moment bringing him nearer to the goal. As the man is led by the Spirit, he bears the fruit of the Spirit—a life filled with love, joy, and peace and surrounded with an atmosphere of patience, kindness, goodness, honesty of purpose, ability to endure affront, and self-control. The Spirit bears fruit in every region of human life. All that fulfills the goal of life by bringing glory to God is of the Spirit.

The chief work that the Holy Spirit has with Christians is to develop them into the likeness of Christ, to reproduce in them the beauty and glory of the personality of Christ. But one cannot develop into the likeness of Christ without bearing the fruit of the Holy Spirit. The test of the Christian life is if it bears the fruit of the Spirit.

In Galatians 5:22-23, the fruit of the Spirit is set forth by the apostle Paul (Also note Romans 5:5; 14:17; 15:13; 2 Corinthians 6:6): "But the fruit of the Spirit is love, joy, peace, patience, kindness, goodness, faithfulness, meekness, self-control; against such there is no law." In this passage, the fruit of the Holy Spirit in the lives of faithful Christians is put in contrast with the works of the flesh. It is as easy to recognize the fruit of the Spirit as it is to recognize the works of the flesh (Matthew 7:16-20). The Christian is characterized by his life in contrast to the life of those of the world. "By their fruits ye shall know them" (Matthew 7:16). All Christians are to bear the same kind of fruit; hence, all Christians are to become like Christ. However, there are some who would profess to be Christians who quench the Holy Spirit (1 Thessalonians 5:19) or grieve the Spirit (Ephesians 4:30). They refuse to be led by the Spirit and, therefore, cannot bear the fruit of the Spirit.

It should be noted that the apostle Paul uses the singular in denoting the fruit of the Spirit. The nine attributes that he lists may thus be referred to as component parts of the "fruit of the Spirit." It cannot be said of anyone that he is truly bearing the fruit of the Spirit, unless he is manifesting each characteristic that comprises that fruit. In other words, one must manifest faithfulness and loving obedience to Christ as well as goodness, kindness, and patience. This is not to say that one must be bearing the fruit of the Spirit to the point of perfection before he can be described as bearing fruit, but he must be striving to that end. It should never be implied that an individual is a fruit-bearing Christian, unless he is actively striving to demonstrate his love for the Lord by yielding his life in obedience to his will. "If you love me, you will obey what I command" (John 14:15).

As the Christian grows in grace and in the knowledge of the truth of God day by day, he will bear the fruit of the Spirit. This growth and development as witnessed in his life is the process of sanctification being accomplished with the aid of the Holy Spirit.

7

THE WORK OF THE HOLY SPIRIT THROUGH THE INSTRUMENTALITY OF THE WRITTEN WORD

A DISTINCTION SHOULD be made between the Holy Spirit and the Word of God. The Holy Spirit is a personality, a member of the Godhead, who dwells in the heart of the faithful Christian. The Word of God, the truth, is an instrument that the Holy Spirit employs. The instrument should not be mistaken for the agent. Although the Holy Spirit is the source of God's Word, there is a difference between the Holy Spirit and the words of the Holy Spirit, even as there is a difference between our words and our spirit. The Holy Spirit uses the instrumentality of the written Word in sanctifying the Christian and enabling him to bear the fruit of the Spirit.

Just as the Holy Spirit uses the Word in the conversion of sinners, so He also uses the Word in the sanctification of the saints. In many instances, the Holy Spirit and the Word of God seem inseparable in that whatever is said of the Holy Spirit is also said of the Word of God. The Christian is born of the Spirit (John 3:5-8) and of the word (I Peter 1:23). We are saved by the Spirit (Titus 3:5) and by the Word (James 1:21). Man is sanctified through the Holy Spirit (1 Corinthians 6:11; 2 Thessalonians 2:13), but Jesus said we are sanctified through the Word (John 17:17). There is power in the Holy Spirit (Romans 15:13), and there is power in the Word (Romans 1:16; Hebrews 1:3). These passages clearly show that the Holy Spirit uses the written Word in accomplishing his work. The Holy Spirit never dispenses with this agency of truth in renewing the hearts of men and guiding Christians in their every walk of life. "Sanctify them in the truth, thy word is truth" (John 17: 17). To the end of sanctifying the Christian and forming Christ in us (Galatians 4:19), the Holy Spirit does several things through the instrumentality of the written Word. He guides and leads the Christian and comforts and encourages him.

THE HOLY SPIRIT GUIDES AND LEADS THROUGH THE WORD

It is through the guidance of the truth that one becomes a Christian, and it is also through continued guidance of God's Word that one develops the Christian life. "For as many as are led by the Spirit of God, these are sons of God" (Romans 8: 14). The Christian is led by the Spirit both externally and internally. Externally, the Spirit supplies the

Gospel truth as set forth in the New Testament, containing the rules and precepts necessary for the instruction and guidance of God's children. When we follow the Word, we are being led by the Spirit. Through the Word, the man of God may be made complete, furnished, completely unto every good work (2 Timothy 3:16: "All scripture is inspired and is useful for teaching, rebuking, correcting, and training in righteousness so that the man of God may be thoroughly equipped for every good work"). To refuse to hear or follow the teachings of the Word is to reject the Spirit and to refuse His guidance.

The Bible is the laws and teachings of the Spirit to guide man. It is the guidebook given to man by the Spirit of God, without which no man can live the Christian life or take a single step toward God and everlasting life. Since man is not able to lead himself (Jeremiah 10:23: "It is not for man to direct his steps." and Proverbs 28:26), it is necessary for man to look to the Word of God for spiritual direction. As man seeks spiritual instruction and guidance he turns to the word of God revealed by the Spirit and takes it into his heart and seeks to mold his thoughts, feelings, purposes, and life by that Holy Word.

> The word of God to man defines the channels through which God's blessings flow and the conditions on which man may enjoy the favor of God. It tells man what conditions of heart, what spiritual frame and what bodily acts manifesting and attesting that frame of heart are essential to the enjoyment of the favor of God. It also furnishes the means and guidance that will produce the conditions of heart and body essential to the enjoyment of divine favor. Through these means provided by

God, the Spirit exerts his influence to instruct, to guide, to strengthen and to comfort.[1]

When the Christian is obedient and faithful to God's Word, it is received into his heart, thus, allowing the Spirit to guide him and lead him in order that his life might bear fruit unto eternal life.

God has chosen his Word as the medium of bestowing and developing spiritual life, and only through the laws of the Spirit, revealed through the word, can spiritual life be imparted, and only through living in accordance with these laws can it be perpetuated and developed. Through the Scriptures inspired of God by his Spirit, the Christian is taught, reproved, corrected, and instructed in the way of righteousness (2 Timothy 3:16). The Word is able to save us (James 1:21) and is capable of building us up in order that we might receive an inheritance of eternal life (Acts 20:31). However, the Spirit can accomplish these ends through the Word, but only when the Christian allows himself to be led by the Spirit, faithfully studying and obeying God's divine will.

THE HOLY SPIRIT COMFORTS AND ENCOURAGES THROUGH THE WORD

In addition to guiding and leading the Christian through the written Word, the Holy Spirit also comforts and encourages the child of God through the Word. "Wherefore comfort one another with these words" (1 Thessalonians 4:18); "For whatsoever things were written aforetime were written for our learning, that through patience and through comfort of the scriptures we might have hope" (Romans 15:4). The Holy Spirit comforts and encourages us by means of the promises and rich blessings He offers us through his Word. The many promises revealed in God's Word provide the hope that exists in the heart of the Christian. The promise of Christ's second coming and the resurrection of the dead was words of comfort to the Thessalonians (I Thessalonians 4:13-18). The promise of Christ's victory over Satan and his hosts were words of comfort to the persecuted Christian (Revelation 17:14: "They will make war against the Lamb, but the Lamb will overcome them because he is Lord of lords and King of kings – and with him will be his called, chosen and faithful followers") and helped give them the courage to endure. A study of the New Testament reveals many promises and blessings that God has made to the faithful Christian. All of these should comfort us and encourage us in our every effort to live a faithful Christian life. The Holy Spirit uses the Word of God to sanctify the Christian, even as He utilizes the Word to convert the alien sinner. Through the instrumentality of the Word, the Holy Spirit guides, leads, and instructs the Christian that he might be furnished completely unto every good work and bear the fruit of the Spirit. The Holy Spirit also comforts and encourages the child of God through the many promises and blessings He has made to us through the Word.

Other passages of comfort and encouragement:

> And we know that in all things God work for the good of those who love him, who have been called according to his purpose.
>
> Romans 8:28

> What shall we say in response to this? If God is for us, who can be against us? He who did not spare his own son, but gave him up for us all – how will

he not also, along with him, graciously give us all things? Who will bring any charge against those whom God as chosen? It is God who justifies. Who is he that condemns? Christ Jesus, who died – more than that, who was raised to life -– is at the right hand of God and is also interceding for us. Who shall separate us from the love of Christ? Shall trouble or hardship or persecution or famine or nakedness or danger or sword? As it is written: For your sake we face death all day long; we are considered as sheep to be slaughtered. No, in all these things we are more than conquerors through him who loved us. For I am convinced that neither death nor life, neither angels nor demons, neither the present nor the future, nor any powers, neither height nor depth, nor anything else in all creation, will be able to separate us from the love of God that is in Christ Jesus our Lord.

Romans 8:31–39

Rejoice in the Lord always. I will say it again: Rejoice. Let your gentleness be evident to all. The Lord is near. Do not be anxious about anything, but in everything by prayer and petitions, with thanksgiving, present your requests to God. And the peace of God, which transcends all understanding, will guard your hearts and your minds in Christ Jesus.

Philippians 4:4–7

Therefore I tell you, do not worry about your life, what you will eat or drink, or about your body, what you will wear. Is not life more important than food, and the body more important than clothes? Look at the birds of the air; they do not sow or reap or store away in barns, and yet your heavenly Father feeds them. Are you not much more valuable than they? Who of you by worrying can add a single hour to his life? And why do you worry about clothes? See how the lilies of the field grow. They do not labor or spin. Yet I tell you that even Solomon, in all his splendor, was dressed like one of these. If that is how God clothes the grass of the field, which is here today and tomorrow is thrown into the fire, will he not much more clothe you, O you of little faith? So do not worry, saying 'What shall we eat?' or What shall we drink?' or 'What shall we wear?' For the pagans run after all these things, and your heavenly Father knows that you need them. But seek first his kingdom and his righteousness, and all these things will be given to you as well. Therefore do not worry about tomorrow, for tomorrow will worry about itself. Each day has enough trouble of its own.

Matthew 6:25–34

Keep your lives free from the love of money and be content with what you have, because God has said, 'Never will I leave you; never will I forsake you.'

Hebrews 13:5

Blessed are the poor in spirit, for theirs is the kingdom of heaven. Blessed are those who mourn, for they will be comforted. Blessed are the meek, for they will inherit the earth. Blessed are those who hunger and thirst for righteousness, for they will be filled. Blessed are the merciful, for they will be shown mercy. Blessed are the pure in heart, for they will see God. Blessed are the peacemakers, for they will be called sons of God. Blessed are those who are persecuted because of righteousness, for theirs is the kingdom of heaven. Blessed are you when people insult you, persecute you and falsely say all kinds of evil against you because of me. Rejoice and be glad, because great is your reward in heaven, for in the same way they persecuted the prophets who were before you.

Matthew 5:3–12

OTHER PASSAGES OF WISDOM

Dear friends, let us love one another, for love comes from God. Everyone who loves has been born of God and knows God. Whoever does not love does not know God, because God is love. This is how God showed his love among us: He sent his one and only Son into the world that we might live through him. This is love: not that we loved God, but that he loves us and sent his Son as an atoning sacrifice for our sins. Dear friends, since God so loved us, we also ought to love one another. No one has ever seen God; but if we love one another, God lives in us and his love is made complete in us. We know that we live in him and he in us, because he has given us of his Spirit. And we have seen and testify that the Father has sent his Son to be the Savior of the world. If anyone acknowledges that Jesus is the Son of God, God lives in him and he in God. And so we know and rely on the love God has for us. God is love. Whoever lives in love lives in God, and God in him. In this way, love is made complete among us so that we will have confidence on the day of judgment, because in this world we are like him. There is no fear in love. But perfect love drives out fear, because fear has to do with punishment. The one who fears is not made perfect in love.

1 John 4:7–18

So in everything, do to others what you would have them do to you, for this sums up the Law and the Prophets.

Matthew 7:12

Love must be sincere. Hate what is evil; cling to what is good. Be devoted to one another in brotherly love. Honor one another above yourselves. Never be lacking in zeal, but keep your spiritual fervor, serving the Lord. Be joyful in hope, patient in affliction, faithful in prayer. Share with God's people who are in need. Practice hospitality. Bless those who persecute you; bless and do not curse. Rejoice with those who rejoice; mourn with those who mourn. Live in harmony with one another. Do not be proud, but be willing to associate with people of low position. Do not be conceited. Do not repay anyone evil for evil. Be careful to do what is right in the eyes of everybody. If it is possible, as far as it depends on you, live at peace with everyone. Do not take revenge, my friends, but leave room for God's wrath, for it is written: It is mine to avenge; I will repay, says the Lord. On the contrary: If your enemy is hungry, feed him; if he is thirsty, give him something to drink, in doing this, you will heap burning coals on his head.

Romans 12:9–21

Obviously, many other passages might be quoted. However, the above passages illustrate the significance of God's Word.

There is no question or challenges you will encounter in life that the Word does not supply an answer or solution to.

The Bible's single theme is "The Salvation of Man." Within its sixty-six books written over 1500 years by, at least, forty authors guided by the Holy Spirit, it is an amazing document.

8

THE GIFT OF
THE HOLY SPIRIT

BEFORE CONSIDERING THE work of the Holy Spirit through the Indwelling Spirit, we first must understand what the Bible says about this gift when we received the Indwelling Spirit and what the Indwelling means.

The New Testament clearly teaches that the Holy Spirit does dwell in the faithful Christian. One of the greatest blessings received by the Christian because of his obedience to the Word of God is the gift of the Holy Spirit. In this chapter, the teachings of the New Testament will be set forth, showing that the Holy Spirit is a gift of God to all those who obey him and that the Spirit dwells in the Christian and must do so in order for one to be a child of God.

THE PROMISE OF ACTS 2:38–39

At the close of Peter's sermon on the day of Pentecost, the multitude of Jews were pricked to the heart, and they asked Peter and the other apostles, "What shall we do?" Peter spoke these words unto them:

> Repent ye, and be baptized every one of you in the name of Jesus Christ unto the remission of your sins; and ye shall receive the gift of the Holy Spirit. For to you is the promise, and to your children, and to all that are afar off, even as many as the Lord our God shall call unto him.
>
> Acts 2:38-39

Thus, it was made known to the world that all those who obeyed the Gospel would receive the blessings of the gift of the Holy Spirit. But just what is this gift, which is promised to the obedient believer? Was this promise of the Holy Spirit for every Christian of every age, or was it a promise of supernatural power to be conferred on a few persons to qualify them to do a work peculiar to the age of miracles as found in the apostolic church? In Hebrews 2:4, the writer, in referring to the work of the apostles, said that God bore witness to them with signs and wonders and by manifold powers and by gifts of the Holy Spirit according to his own will. In 1 Corinthians 12, Paul enumerates nine different spiritual gifts, all of which partook of the miraculous gifts and were bestowed upon the apostles and certain other Christians in the early church. Were these miraculous gifts of the Holy Spirit mentioned in Hebrews 2 and 1 Corinthians 12 the "gift of the Holy Spirit" to which Peter referred in Acts 2:38?

> Not a promise of a miraculous outpouring of the
> Spirit, but a promise of the Holy Spirit Himself.

That the "gift of the Holy Spirit" in Acts 2:38 was not the miraculous spiritual gifts of 1 Corinthians 12 can be seen by the following observations. The "gift of the Holy Spirit" in Acts 2:38 is promised to the same ones who are promised the remission of sins. The gift was promised to all who heard and obeyed Peter's commandments (Acts 2:39). However, it is known from the subsequent history of the church that spiritual gifts were not bestowed on all who repented and were baptized but on only a few brethren in each of the several congregations (Note 1 Corinthians 12). If the gift of the Holy Spirit were the spiritual gifts conferred through the laying on of the apostles' hands, then all the three thousand baptized on Pentecost received a miraculous gift of the Holy Spirit enabling them to perform miracles. But there is no evidence that anyone, other than the apostles, enjoyed any extraordinary gift until after the apostles laid their hands upon the seven men in Acts 6.

As disciples of Christ, Stephen, Philip, and the other five had the gift of the Holy Spirit (Acts 6:3), and, as assistants of the apostles, they had the power to perform miracles (Acts 6:8; 8:6). Also, as was previously noted, spiritual gifts were obtained only through the laying on of the apostles' hands. There is no indication in Acts 2 that it was necessary for the apostles to lay their hands upon those who repented and were baptized before they could receive the Holy Spirit. Another consideration concerning the gift of the Holy Spirit is that it is obviously intended to continue to be given as long as it is the remission of sins (Acts 2:39). If this be true, then the "gift of the Holy Spirit" could not possibly refer to the spiritual gifts since they ceased with the apostolic period of the church. Another observation is that in Acts 2:38, the word *gift* is singular. When spiritual or miraculous powers are meant to be plural, *gifts* is always used (1 Corinthians 12:4, 9, 28, 30, 31). Thus, the "gift of the Holy Spirit" does not mean "spiritual gifts." The gift of Acts 2:38 is the Holy Spirit Himself given and not merely the power with which He invests a person for special purposes.

Another line of reasoning, which is occasionally set forth, is that the "gift of the Holy Spirit" in Acts 2:38 is equal to the action of the Holy Spirit received by the apostles on Pentecost (Acts 2:1-4) and by the household of Cornelius (Acts 10:44-46). In support of this view, it is noted that the only other place in the New Testament besides Acts 2:38 where the phrase "gift of the Holy Spirit" is used is in Acts 10:45, when Cornelius and his household received the Holy Spirit. However, there is one fact that clearly distinguishes the "gift of the Holy Spirit" from the household of Cornelius. In the latter case, the gift of the Spirit was manifested by the miracle of speaking in tongues, and certainly not everyone who repented and was baptized was given the ability to speak with tongues (1 Corinthians 14). Also, it is noted that Cornelius and his house received this gift of the Holy Spirit prior to their water baptism, while Peter makes baptism a necessary condition for the reception of the "gift of the Holy Spirit" in Acts 2:38. It is clearly seen, therefore, that the promise of the Holy Spirit in Acts 2 was neither spiritual gifts nor similar to the Spirit's action in Acts 2:1–4 and Acts 10. The "gift of the Holy Spirit" is not a miraculous outpouring of the Spirit but the Spirit himself given to the obedient believer.

THE INDWELLING SPIRIT

The true meaning of the "gift of the Holy Spirit" can be seen from a study of the New Testament passages teaching that the Holy Spirit has been given to the Christian and dwells within him. In Paul's letter to the church at Rome, there are several passages which show that the Holy Spirit dwells in the Christian. "The love of God hath been shed abroad in our hearts through the Holy Spirit which was given unto us" (Romans 5:5). Again, "But if the Spirit of him that raised up Christ Jesus from the dead dwells in you, he who raised Christ Jesus from the dead shall give life also to your mortal bodies through his Spirit that dwells in you" (Romans 8:11). And then in Paul's first epistle to the Corinthians, "Or know you not that your body is a temple of the Holy Spirit which is in you, which you have from God? and you are not your own" (1 Corinthians 6:19).

JESUS'S TEACHING ON THE INDWELLING SPIRIT

The above passages harmonize with Jesus's promise to his disciples. The Holy Spirit was promised as an abiding guest and comforter, and as such was to dwell with them and be in them forever. "And I will pray the Father, and he shall give you another Comforter, that he may be with you forever, even the Spirit of truth whom the world cannot receive; for it beholds him not, neither knows him: you know him; for he abides with you and shall be in you" (John 14:16-17).

This abiding of the Spirit was not figurative, but a literal indwelling of the Holy Spirit as seen from Acts 2:1–4. Since the Holy Spirit was literally in the apostles to inspire them, He was also literally in the apostles to comfort them.

It may be argued that the promise of the abiding Spirit as a comforter was to the apostles only and, since they were inspired by His presence, the absence of such inspiration proves the absence of the Spirit. However, a careful examination of the Scriptures will show that while there was no promise that the inspiration should remain, as a comforter He was to abide forever (John 14:17). If this promise was to the apostles only, then why did Jesus promise that He should abide with them forever? Certainly they were not to live forever on earth, and after death they were to be with the Lord again and would not need the Comforter.

Earlier in the fourth Gospel, John said that the Holy Spirit would be received by those who believed in him, including more than the apostles, "But this spoke he of the Spirit, which they that believed on him were to receive: for the Spirit was not yet given; because Jesus was not yet glorified" (John 7:39). The Comforter continues to dwell in the faithful Christian, and, while He has fulfilled His mission as an inspiring guide, He abides forever as a comforter.

OTHER NEW TESTAMENT PASSAGES THAT TEACH THE POSSESSION OF THE HOLY SPIRIT BY THE CHRISTIAN

In addition to the passages already set forth, there are several others that show that the Christian possesses the Holy Spirit. "And because ye are sons, God sent forth the Spirit of his Son into our hearts, crying Abba, Father" (Galatians 4:6). Here Paul states the fact that not only has God given us his Spirit but also that he has done so because we are his children. The Christian has received the Holy Spirit as a seal, "And grieve not the Holy Spirit of God, in whom ye were sealed unto the day of redemption" (Ephesians 4:30; cf. Ephesians 1:13). He has also received the Spirit as an earnest of his inheritance, "Now he that wrought us for this very thing is God, who gave unto us the earnest of the Spirit" (2 Corinthians 5:5; also 1 Corinthians 1:22; Ephesians 1:13-14; Romans 8:23). In Ephesians 5:18, Paul exhorts the Ephesians to be "filled with the Spirit," which implies that it was possible for them to have the Spirit. In an exhortation to Timothy, Paul says that the Holy Spirit dwells in us, "That good thing which was committed unto you guard through the Holy Spirit which dwells in us" (2 Timothy 1:14).

In the epistle to Titus, Paul states, "According to his mercy he saved us, through the washing of regeneration and renewing of the Holy Spirit, which he poured out upon us richly, through Jesus Christ our Savior" (Titus 3:5-6). The Holy Spirit is freely given to those who have been baptized into Christ. God is the source of the Holy Spirit, which is given to us, "Therefore he that rejects, rejects not man, but God who gives his Holy Spirit unto you" (1 Thessalonians 4:8; cf. Acts 5:32). John says that we may know that God abides in us by the Spirit, which he has given to us (1 John 3:24). It can be seen in the light of the above passages that the Holy Spirit does, indeed, dwell within the Christian.

EXAMPLES OF THE INDWELLING SPIRIT

In the New Testament, there are two expressions that might imply the indwelling of the Holy Spirit in particular individuals or groups. These are: "full of the Holy Spirit" and "being filled with the Holy Spirit." The former is used five times and the latter ten times in the New Testament. For the most part, these expressions seem to have been limited to the days of Christ and the early church and refer to the miraculous outpouring of the Holy Spirit on various individuals. However, there are six times that these expressions are used in which they do not imply the miraculous but indicate that the early Christian possessed the indwelling Spirit separately and apart from any spiritual gifts.

In Acts 6, seven men were to be selected to oversee a certain phase of the church's work. They were to be "full of the Spirit" (v. 3), and Stephen, one of the seven, was specifically said to be "full of the Holy Spirit" (v. 5). It is noted that these men possessed the Holy Spirit prior to the laying on of the apostles' hands, therefore, being "full of the Holy Spirit" could not refer to their possession of spiritual gifts. This is the first time the expression "full of the Spirit or Holy Spirit" is used in the New Testament when it does not obviously refer to a miraculous manifestation of the Holy Spirit. It could only mean that Stephen and the other six men had the gift or indwelling of the Holy Spirit, as was promised by Peter in Acts 2:38 to all those who obeyed the gospel. The evidence that showed that the Spirit dwelt within them was the fruits of a holy life.

In Acts 9, there is an account of the apostle Paul's conversion. Chapter 9, verse 17 reads: "And Ananias departed and entered into the house; and laying his hands on him, he said, Brother Saul, the Lord, even Jesus, who appeared unto you in the way which you came, hath sent me, that you may receive your sight, and be filled with the Holy Spirit."

Since only the apostles had the power to bestow spiritual gifts, Ananias would have been unable to give Paul any spiritual gift. Therefore, for Paul to be filled with the Holy Spirit could only refer to the "gift of the Holy Spirit." And it follows that Paul received the Spirit after he was baptized by Ananias (Acts 9:18).

This made his reception of the Holy Spirit dependent on the coming of Ananias, and it sufficiently accounts for the words of the latter, without resorting to the improbable supposition that he was empowered to do that which none but apostles could ordinarily do.[1]

In Acts 11:24, Luke describes Barnabas as being a good man and full of the Holy Spirit and of faith. Since there is no indication that Barnabas at this time could perform miracles, it is possible that the phrase "full of the Holy Spirit" in this verse could refer to the ordinary indwelling of the Spirit. In Acts 13:52, Paul and Barnabas were said to be "filled with joy and with the Holy Spirit." The context does not seem to infer a miraculous gift, so here again the indwelling of the Holy Spirit may well be meant. Neither of these last two examples is as conclusive as the first two, but the gift of the Holy Spirit does seem to be implied rather than the miraculous manifestation of the Spirit.

The last example is found in Ephesians 5:18 where Paul exhorted the Ephesians to be filled with the Holy Spirit. Obviously, spiritual gifts are not meant in this passage, since all were exhorted to be "filled with" the Spirit, which means to use fully the Spirit that you already possess. This verse would, of necessity, then refer to the indwelling of the Holy Spirit promised to all Christians. In this passage, Paul is making a contrast between the man who is drunk with wine, and the man who is filled with the Spirit. The former's life is characterized by riot, while the Christian's life should be distinguished by the singing of spiritual songs and prayer—a result of the Christian's allowing himself to be filled or led by the Spirit.

9

THE RECEPTION OF THE HOLY SPIRIT BY THE CHRISTIAN

THE GIFT OF indwelling of the Holy Spirit was a new promise, which God had never before given to man. While the Spirit had been active in the Patriarchal and Mosaic dispensations He had never been promised to the faithful followers of God in any of the old covenants. But to all those of the Christian dispensation who will obey the commands of God, this exceedingly great promise of the Holy Spirit is theirs.

THE ABSENCE OF THE INDWELLING SPIRIT PRIOR TO THE NEW COVENANT

The coming of the Holy Spirit or Comforter to dwell in the hearts of the people of God was a new thing, peculiar to the Christian dispensation. There is not the least evidence in the Old Testament that the Spirit dwelt in the children of God in that age, except in those who performed some miraculous feat or who were inspired with God by the Holy Spirit to reveal his divine will. In Old Testament passages that refer to the Spirit imparting moral and spiritual character, they are in each case a prophecy concerning the action of the Spirit in the approaching kingdom of God.

> For I will pour water upon him that is thirsty, and floods upon the dry ground: I will pour my spirit upon thy seed, and my blessing upon thine offspring: and they shall spring up as among the grass, as willows by the water courses. One shall say, I am the Lord's; and another shall call himself by the name of Jacob and another shall subscribe with his hand unto the Lord, and surname himself by the name of Israel.
>
> Isaiah 44:3-5

One of the greatest promises concerning the future work of the Spirit is found in Ezekiel 36:26-28.

> A new heart also will I give you, and a new spirit will I put within you: and I will take away the stony heart out of your flesh, and I will give you an heart of flesh. And I will put my Spirit within you, and cause you to walk in my statutes, and ye shall keep my judgments, and do them. And ye shall dwell in

the land that I gave to your fathers and ye shall be my people, and I will be your God.

Although the Holy Spirit was active in several ways during the Old Testament period, He did not personally dwell in the individual hearts of God's people. The absence of such an activity of the Spirit was noted earlier in the study of the Holy Spirit in the Old Testament. The distinction between the work of the Holy Spirit in the former dispensations and the present Christian era has been stated as thus:

> In the old dispensation the Holy Spirit wrought upon believers but did not in his person dwell in believers and abide permanently in them. He appeared unto men; he did not incarnate himself in man. His action was intermittent; he went and came like the dove which Noah sent forth from the ark, and which went to and fro, finding no rest; while in the new dispensation he dwells, he abides in the heart as the dove, his emblem which John saw descending and alighting on the head of Jesus. Affianced of the soul, the Spirit went off to see his betrothed, but was not yet one with her; the marriage was not consummated until the Pentecost after the glorification of Jesus Christ.[1]

When Jesus became the mediator of a new and better covenant, he purposed it as a better covenant by the granting of new blessings not enjoyed before, such as the full remission of sins and the indwelling of the Holy Spirit. That the believer did not possess the Holy Spirit until after the new covenant was established is evident from John 7:39, "But this spoke he of the Spirit, which they that believed on him were to receive: for the Spirit was not yet given; because Jesus was not yet glorified."

After the Holy Spirit came in fulfillment of Jesus's promise to the apostles (John 14-16), He maintained a relationship to the apostles and to those who had spiritual gifts similar to the relationship He had had with Old Testament writers and prophets and with those men of Old Testament days who had been able to perform miraculous feats. However, the Spirit maintained a new relationship to the children of God, since He dwelt in the heart of every faithful Christian. This "gift of the Holy Spirit" possessed by the Christian had never been received before.

CONDITIONS TO BE MET IN ORDER TO OBTAIN THE PROMISE OF THE HOLY SPIRIT

As has already been noted, the "gift of the Holy Spirit" promised by Peter on the day of Pentecost was given to those who repented and were baptized. In another place, Peter said that the Holy Spirit was given by God to those that obey him (Acts 5:32). It seems evident from these passages that obedience to the Gospel is necessary before one can receive the Holy Spirit. The Spirit does not come to those of the world, "even the Spirit of truth; whom the world cannot receive; for it beholds him not, neither knows him" (John 14:17). "The Spirit does not enter the heart before its purification. There can be no communion between light and darkness--Christ and the devil. The Holy Spirit enters the heart of man after it has been purified by the blood of Christ and the body of sin destroyed."[2]

From the moment of baptism, the life of the Spirit in the Christian begins. In Luke 11:13, Jesus said that the Father gives the Spirit to such of his children as ask him for it. This statement does not mean that man has no conditions with which to comply before he can receive the Spirit. God also gives us our bread, and Jesus taught his disciples to pray for it, yet man must still do his part. Man must also do his part before he can receive the gift of the Holy Spirit. The Holy Spirit, like every good gift, may be asked for. "The earnest desire and petition for God's gifts is an essential preparation for receiving and enjoying them."[3] When a man has a true and sincere desire for something, he will pray for it and do that which is necessary to obtain it.

Another statement concerning the way in which the Holy Spirit is received is found in Galatians 3:2, "Received ye the Spirit by the works of the law, or by the hearing of faith?" Two thoughts are implied by this verse: first, that the Galatians did not receive the Holy Spirit by the works of the law; and second, that they did receive it by the hearing of faith. But what is the hearing of faith? In this chapter, the apostle Paul is evidently contrasting the Mosaic Law to the Gospel. Hence, the word *faith* in this verse is synonymous to the Gospel system and comprehends the whole plan of salvation presented in the Gospel. The word *hearing* in this verse evidently means something more than the reception of sound.

The word used here implies obedience in other passages such as Acts 3:23, "And it shall be, that every soul that shall not hearken to that prophet, shall be utterly destroyed from among the people." Note, also, Romans 1:5 where Paul says, "We received grace and apostleship to call people from among all the Gentiles to the obedience that comes from faith." Thus, the passage may be read that the Galatians received the Holy Spirit by their obedience to the Gospel or by expressing their faith by obedience. The reception of the Spirit in Galatians 3:2 could not have reference to any miraculous endowment of the Holy Spirit because that came through the laying on of apostles' hands and not "by the hearing of faith."

Obedience to the Gospel is, thus, the condition that must be met before the Holy Spirit is received. One must become a citizen of the kingdom of God and a member of God's family. Not until then can the Spirit be received, which entitles us to the privilege of calling God our Father. Only adopted sons of God may obtain the gift of the Holy Spirit. "And because ye are sons, God sent forth the Spirit of his Son into our hearts, crying, Abba, Father" (Galatians 4:6).

Since the reception of the Holy Spirit is dependent upon our obedience to God's will, the inference is irresistible that the measure of our enjoyment of the Holy Spirit is not a fixed quantity but that it will depend on the perfection of our faith in Christ and our love for him. The more faithful a Christian is, the more the Spirit of Christ benefits him. The more consecrated a Christian is, the richer and fuller will be the blessings of the Holy Spirit.

> The Holy Spirit comes into the Christian's heart and consciousness along the lines of love, sympathy, and personal trust. If the love of God for us, as manifested in Christ, Jesus, awakens a responsive love for God in the human heart, along this line of reciprocal affection God sends his Spirit, and with him the richest treasures of his grace and truth, and we are filled with all the fullness of God.

But if God's love evokes no answering affection in
our heart, if it breaks down no barriers of alienation
and distrust, this absence of reciprocity prevents the
inflow of the divine power and life into the human
soul, and leaves it barren and unfruitful.[4]

We conclude that the extent to which the Christian
seeks after God and serves him will determine the extent
to which he receives the blessings of the indwelling of the
Holy Spirit.

10

THE WORK OF THE INDWELLING SPIRIT AS A COMFORTER

IT HAS BEEN noted in previous chapters that the Holy Spirit dwells within the faithful Christian. The Holy Spirit is given by God to those who obey him (Acts 5:32). The indwelling Spirit in the heart of the Christian works toward the end of sanctifying the child of God. It is this phase of the Spirit's work that is unique, for never before has the individual man "possessed the Holy Spirit" for the purpose of aiding him to live a righteous and godlike life. It is a blessing promised only to the Christian (Acts 2:38-39). It is in the sphere of the human spirit that the Holy Spirit is truly able to work in and for the Christian to enable him to bear the fruit of the Spirit.

The Spirit accomplishes much for the Christian through the instrumentality of the written Word, but the distinctive work that He does as He dwells within the heart of the Christian cannot be accomplished through the Word. Through the indwelling Spirit, the whole of man is affected—his mind, his body, his emotions, and his spirit. Just as the Holy Spirit worked in several ways through the instrumentality of the Word, so He also works in several ways to sanctify the Christian as He dwells within him. The indwelling Spirit comforts, strengthens, and makes intercession for the child of God.

> You shall receive the Holy Spirit as a gift; it shall enter into you and hence be in you, according to the Master's promise; it shall dwell in you as its fitting earthly temple; to which let us add, as consequences, it shall comfort you, so that you shall not evermore carry in your hearts the lonely, disconsolate feeling of orphans; it shall strengthen you with strength in the feeble inner man; it shall intercede for you in the sighs which no human speech can express, to procure for you such things as you know not how to pray for as you should—such shall be the gift of the Spirit in you, and such shall it be to you.[1]

THE INDWELLING SPIRIT COMFORTS

Previously, we have noted that Jesus promised his apostles the Comforter, even the Spirit of truth who would abide in them (John 14:16-17). But as it was observed, the Spirit's mission as a comforter was not limited to the apostles but included all faithful Christians in whom the Spirit dwells in fulfillment of the Lord's promise (John 7:39). We shall see that the Holy Spirit is active as a comforter as He dwells within the heart of the Christian as well as being a comforter through the written Word.

The Indwelling Spirit comforts the child of God in at least five ways:

1. As a representative of God and Christ.

2. As a proof of sonship.

3. As an earnest payment or pledge.

4. As a seal.

5. Bearing witness with our spirit that we are children of God.

AS A REPRESENTATIVE OF GOD AND CHRIST

> No man hath beheld God at any time: if we love one another, God abides in us, and his love is perfected in us; hereby we know that we abide in him and he in us, because he hath given us of his Spirit. And we have beheld and bear witness that the Father hath sent the Son to be the Savior of the world. Whosoever shall confess that Jesus is the Son of God, God abides in him; and he in God.
>
> 1 John 4:12–15

In 2 Corinthians 6:16, Paul writes, "Even as God said, I will dwell in them and walk in them; and I will be their God and they shall be my people." It is also said that Christ dwells in us: "That Christ may dwell in your hearts through faith" (Ephesians 3:17). But God is in his heaven, and Christ is at the right hand of God. He has ascended back to the Father. Therefore, neither one dwells in the Christian personally. Then how do God and Christ dwell in us? They dwell in us through their representative, the Holy Spirit. After Christ ascended back to the Father, they sent the Holy Spirit to the apostles and to the Church (John 15:26). The Holy Spirit represents God and Christ on earth. When the Holy Spirit dwells in Christians, God and Christ dwell in them.

That the Holy Spirit does represent God and Christ in the heart of the Christian can be seen from the following observations. The Spirit is not only referred to as the Holy Spirit, but He is also called the Spirit of God and the Spirit of Christ. "But ye are not in the flesh but in the Spirit, if so be that the Spirit of God dwells in you. But if any man hath not the Spirit of Christ he is none of his" (Romans 8:9; see also 1 Corinthians 3:16; 1 Peter 1:10-11; 2 Peter 2:21). These passages show that the terms "Spirit of Christ," "Spirit of God," and the "Holy Spirit" all refer to the same person and are only different ways of referring to the Spirit. But because He is referred to as the Spirit of God and the Spirit of Christ, it is evident that He is representative of them. It is also noted that in the passage quoted above (1 John 4:12-15) John states that we know God abides in us because he has given us his Spirit. The Christian that has the Holy Spirit knows that God abides in him. The Spirit is God's representative in the Christian (Note also 1 John 3:24).

Another passage that shows God is represented by the Holy Spirit is Ephesians 2:22, "In whom ye also are built together for a habitation of God in the Spirit." The saints in Ephesus composed a habitation or place to dwell, and in it God dwelt in the Spirit. But God did not dwell in the habitation in person but representatively through his Spirit. "The Holy Spirit dwelt in the saints in Ephesus, and by it, as representing him, God dwelt in them."[2]

The Holy Spirit during the Christian era is "in office" on earth, and all spiritual presence and divine communion of the Trinity with men are through Him. In other words, while the Father and Son are personally in heaven, they are on earth in the body of the faithful by the indwelling of the Comforter. The Christian may know that the abiding fellowship of God with man and of man with God becomes a matter of personal knowledge through his possession of the Spirit of God. For the indwelling of the Spirit of God in man is the indwelling of God himself. It is by his Spirit that God dwells and works in us.

As a Proof of Sonship

The New Testament teaches that the indwelling Spirit is a proof to the Christian that he is a son of God. In Galatians 4:6, Paul said, "And because ye are sons, God hath sent forth the Spirit of his Son into your hearts, crying Abba, Father." The Spirit was not given to make them sons but because they were sons. Thus, when the Holy Spirit dwells in our hearts, it is proof that God has accepted us as sons. In fact, if a man does not have the Spirit of Christ, he is not a Christian. Paul makes the possession of the Holy Spirit on the part of the believer to be the test of genuine discipleship. "But if any man hath not the Spirit of Christ, he is none of his" (Romans 8:9). The possession of the Holy Spirit brings a feeling of assurance to the child of God, a feeling that is increased by the communion of the Holy Spirit. "The grace of the Lord Jesus Christ and the love of God and the communion of the Holy Spirit, be with you all" (2 Corinthians 13:14).

The purpose of the Son's mission to earth was to make possible the rights of sonship. The purpose of the Spirit's mission is to give the power of using them. The Spirit of Christ is sent into the hearts of adopted sons because he is the very "Spirit of sonship." The possession of the Holy Spirit is the distinguishing badge, the peculiar characteristic of the Christian. It is that which sets him apart from the world. Because he has the gift of the Holy Spirit, he may know assuredly that he is a son of God.

As a Seal

In 2 Corinthians and Ephesians, Paul taught that the Christian is sealed by the Holy Spirit. "In whom, having also believed, ye were sealed with the Holy Spirit of promise." (Ephesians 1:13). In 2 Corinthians 1:21-22, it states, "Now he that established us with you in Christ and anointed us, is God: who also sealed us, and gave us the earnest of the Spirit in our hearts" (See also Ephesians 4:30).

A seal, anciently as now, was an official mark put upon any document to authenticate it or indicate its genuineness. A seal is also a mark of ownership or possession. And finally, a seal is a means of security: The fact that the Christian receives the Holy Spirit and is thereby sealed proves three things. The Christian has a mark of character, a stamp of genuineness put upon him by the Holy Spirit, a true sign to the world of his discipleship. The person who is filled with the Spirit bears the stamp of the Spirit. His behavior—words, dress, train of ideas, interests, everything that he does, says, and is—bears the stamp of God. Second, it is proof that he belongs to God. The Christian has indisputable evidence that he is God's beloved, one with Christ, united to him, saved in him, with an everlasting salvation. Third, it is a proof of the Christian's security. With the seal, he is a true child of God. It is a guarantee of all God's covenanted promises and of all the heavenly blessings he has prepared for those who love and serve him.

While many have tried to parallel baptism and circumcision, arguing that as circumcision was the seal or sign that one was in the covenant, so in Christianity baptism is the seal that one is a child of God, there is no indication in the New Testament that baptism has ever been considered as a sign or seal of covenant relationship with God. On the other hand, it is quite evident that the gift of the Holy Spirit comes in the room of circumcision. "It was fleshly birth that made one a Jew, and circumcision was the seal or sign that one was in the covenant. In Christianity, by analogy, baptism is the time of the new birth, and the gift of the Holy Spirit is the sign of membership in the covenant.[3] As the uncircumcised was to be cut off from his people (Genesis 17:14), one who does not have the Spirit of Christ also does not belong to him (Romans 8:9). He lacks the seal of a covenant relationship with God.

As an Earnest or Pledge?

In the same passages that teach that the Christian is sealed by the Holy Spirit, Paul describes the Spirit as the earnest of the future life. "In whom, having also believed, ye were sealed with the Holy Spirit of promise, which is an earnest of our inheritance unto the redemption of God's own possession, unto the praise of his glory" (Ephesians 1:13-14). And in 2 Corinthians 5:5, "Now he that wrought us for this very thing is God, who gave unto us the earnest of the Spirit" (Also 2 Corinthians 1:22). In human transactions, an earnest is a deposit or a pledge of full payment.

In like manner, God has guaranteed immortal life to the Christian by his gift of the Spirit, which makes us partakers, even now, of divine privileges. The possession of the Spirit is a promise or pledge of a fuller and richer future; of an inheritance to be received in the life to come. However, to have received the Spirit is not only a cause for thankfulness but is also a source of increased responsibility. The first installment of spiritual life, which the Spirit brings, is not an absolute guarantee of final deliverance; it makes for that end, but it may be frustrated by the conduct of the person who has received the Spirit. The Spirit works in the heart of the Christian to prepare him for the full inheritance when the time shall come to receive it. The child of God has only to let himself be led by the Spirit (Romans 8:14).

A passage very similar in meaning to those above is Romans 8:23, "And not only so, but ourselves also, who have the first- fruits of the Spirit, even we ourselves groan within ourselves, waiting for our adoption, to wit, the redemption of our body." The phrase "first fruits of the Spirit" seems to imply the same meaning as the "earnest of the Spirit." Paul is saying that the Spirit in us is but the first fruits of the future great harvest of spiritual life our adoption has been, as yet only in part, for the body is still subject to death and the tendency to sin. But the day of redemption will come, and the Christian will then enjoy the complete fulfillment (Ephesians 4:30).

Bearing Witness with Our Spirit

In Romans 8:16, Paul says, "The Spirit himself bears witness with our spirit, that we are children of God." The apostle speaks here of two witnesses—the Holy Spirit and our spirit. If we are led by the Holy Spirit (verse 14), then He unites with our spirit to testify that we are God's children. This testimony is for the purpose of assuring and confirming our own faith. The witness of the Spirit with our spirits takes away the doubts and fears that adversity brings. The witness of the Spirit with our spirit occurs after conversion and assures the believer that he is a member of the family of God. It is not testimony that is given once, but it occurs throughout the Christian's life as he is led by the Spirit. In fact, it is in our being led by the Spirit that both our spirit and the indwelling Spirit bear witness to our being children of God.

The testimony of the Spirit is that we are led by Him and therefore are children of God. He bears witness to this effect when we allow ourselves to be led by Him. The Spirit of God leads both externally and internally—externally through the Word and internally through the indwelling Spirit as He strengthens the inner man. (The internal leading of the Spirit is discussed more fully in the next chapter.) As the Christian faithfully follows God's Word and allows himself to be strengthened by the indwelling Spirit, he becomes more able to overcome sin and to bear the fruit of the Spirit. When the fruit of the Spirit is manifested in the life of the Christian, it is evident that he is being led by the Spirit. The result of the Spirit's leading, the fruit of the Spirit, makes it possible for the Spirit to testify that we are children of God. As the Christian allows himself to be led by the Spirit, he will bear the fruit of the Spirit. In this manner, the Spirit testifies that he is a son of God.

To the witness of the Spirit, the testimony of our own spirits is added. Our spirits can testify whether we are allowing ourselves to be led by the Word of God and by the indwelling Spirit or quenching and resisting the Spirit. The Christian knows whether or not he is bearing the fruit of the Spirit.

> We know within ourselves what our spiritual state is, what our wish, intent, and effort are. Are these in strict accordance with the Father's will as read in his word? Are we living closely up to his will, and holding the evil inclinations of the flesh in check? Are we keeping the body under? Over all its perverse tendencies is a spirit, enlightened and pure, dominant? All this we know within ourselves, and to it can testify.[4]

Thus, both our spirit and the Holy Spirit testify that we are children of God, as we are led by the Spirit and the fruit of the Spirit is evidenced in our lives.

> If we are led, we know it, and so our own spirit testifies to us. If we are led in the godly, spiritual path, it can be none other than the Holy Spirit who leads; and so, in the very act of leading, the Spirit testifies to us. And lastly, if we are led, and if we follow, this union of our spirit and God's Spirit in joint action proves us children of God.[5]

Once again, the Christian can be assured that he is a son of God because of the Holy Spirit that dwells within his heart and, by this knowledge, be comforted and encouraged in striving to live a Christlike life.

What is the significance of our understanding the five ways the Spirit comforts us? First of all, we can be assured that we belong to God and our salvation is assured. We need not fear that we are in a covenant relationship with God. Romans 8:15 assures us that "we have not received a spirit that makes you a slave again to fear, but you receive the spirit of sonship." God wants us to feel confident about our salvation and our relationship to Him.

Secondly, each of the ways the Holy Spirit comforts us is an indication of God's love. He longs to be a part of our lives, working in us and through us to carry out His will.

One final note regarding the fruit of the Spirit is God's way of testifying that we are his children. It is well for us to take an inventory once in a while. We need to ask ourselves the question, "Am I growing in love? Am I more loving now than I was five years ago? Is there more joy in my heart than there was five years ago? Am I more at peace with myself than I was before? Do I see kindness and goodness reflected in my life? Am I growing in patience? Am I faithful? Am I loyal?" No, I'm not perfect, but am I growing in these areas? My growth as a Christian will be measured by Christlike characteristics. As I grow spiritually, the greater my confidence is that I am a child of God.

11

THE WORK OF THE HOLY SPIRIT AS A SOURCE OF STRENGTH

THE GREATEST WORK of the indwelling Spirit is His strengthening of the inward man. Paul speaks of this work of the Spirit in his letter to the Ephesians.

> For this cause I bow my knees unto the Father, from whom every family in heaven and on earth is named, that he would grant you, according to the riches of his glory, that ye may be strengthened with power through his Spirit in the inward man that Christ may dwell in your hearts through faith, to the end that ye being rooted and grounded in love, may be strong to apprehend with all the saints what is the breadth and length and height and depth, and to know the love of Christ which passes knowledge, that ye may be filled unto all the fullness of God.

> Now to him who is able to do immeasurably more than all we ask or imagine, according to his power that is at work within us.
>
> Ephesians 3:14-20

In Philippians 4:13, the apostle writes, "I can do all things in him that strengthens me." These passages show that God strengthens the Christian, and Ephesians 3:16 states that he does so through the Spirit dwelling within him.

In Paul's prayer for the Ephesians quoted above (Ephesians 3:14-19), we see that the goal of the Christian life is "the fullness of God" (verse 19). But this end is not obtained until the Christian is made strong through being rooted and grounded in love, a fruit of the Spirit. The obtaining of this love is a result of Christ's dwelling in the Christian's heart through faith, which, in turn, is dependent upon the Spirit's dwelling in the inward man (verses 16-17). In this progress toward being filled with "all the fullness of God," the human nature alone is insufficient. Behind it all, there lies a strengthening of the will and the whole spiritual nature or "inner man" by the Spirit of God (verse 16). Spiritual strength is a primary and most fundamental need of human nature on its way to God. Without this strength obtained through the indwelling Spirit, no man would be able to live the Christian life.

> Without this gift (the gift of the Holy Spirit) no one could be saved or ultimately triumph over all opposition. Man himself is not competent to wrestle against the allied forces of the world, flesh and the devil. But by his Holy Spirit, in answer to our prayers, God works in us, and by us and for us, all that is needful to our present, spiritual and eternal salvation.[1]

It is only with the help of the Spirit of God dwelling within us that we can fashion ourselves to the image of the Lord that is set before us. The spiritual strength that is obtained from the indwelling Spirit is indispensably necessary to living the Christian life and for overcoming the flesh and the many temptations the child of God encounters. In living a Christian life, it is necessary that the flesh be overcome, that sin be subdued and no longer have dominion over the child of God (Romans 6:6, 14). The Spirit of God who dwells only in the Christian comes in contact with the flesh, and, by the Spirit's assistance, the tempting power in the flesh is overcome.

The habits of life become transformed as the Spirit gradually helps us overcome the adversary so that the works of the flesh are displaced by the fruit of the Spirit. When the "works of flesh" are carefully compared with the "fruit of the Spirit" as described by Paul in Galatians 5:19-23, the deadly antagonism between the two categories is realized, and there can be no doubt that only as one possesses the Holy Spirit can he overcome the one class and bring forth the other in his life. The Christian then is able to mortify and crucify the flesh by the Holy Spirit that dwells within him and strengthens him. Without this strength afforded by the indwelling Spirit, the Christian would be overcome by the flesh and by temptation, unable to endure and, therefore, subject to eternal death.

The above picture is clearly set forth by the apostle Paul in the seventh and eighth chapters of Romans. This passage shows the helplessness of man under any form of law. The law cannot change a man's nature and, therefore, cannot save him from himself. God, in his system of grace, provides the way for the change in man's nature so that the sinful nature in him can be overcome, and his spiritual, regenerate nature is left free to serve God in righteousness.

The author's primary concern in the first eight chapters of Romans is man and his relationship to sin. In chapters 1 to 3, the apostle affirms and clearly illustrates that all men, both Gentiles and Jews, are guilty of sin. In Romans 3:23, we read: "For all have sinned and fall short of the glory of God." Sinful man stands before God without hope. "For the wages of sin is death" (Romans 6:23). Man is in a most pitiful condition in that he cannot justify himself by any manner of law-keeping or works of merit. "Because by the work of the law shall no flesh be justified in his sight" (Romans 3:20). Then, to the man without hope, Paul presents the solution to mankind's dilemma in the person of Jesus Christ. We are "justified freely by his grace through the redemption that is in Jesus Christ" (Romans 3:24). In order for man to overcome the guilt of sin, he is dependent on the grace of God as expressed in the blood of Christ. "But God commends his own love toward us, in that, while we were yet sinners, Christ died for us. Much more then, being now justified by his blood shall we be saved from the wrath of God through him" (Romans 5:8–9).

To become the beneficiary of Christ's great sacrifice, Paul teaches that man must respond to God in accordance with the principle of faith. In Romans 5:1, we read: "Being therefore justified by faith, we have peace with God through our Lord Jesus Christ." This faith principle encompasses not only a belief in Jesus Christ but also a trust in the power of his blood (Romans 3:25) and a yielding in humble obedience to the Lord's command that we be baptized (Romans 6:3–4).

Paul is not only concerned with sin from the standpoint of man's guilt; he is equally concerned with the problem of man overcoming the domination or control of sin in his daily life. It is to this point that Paul addresses himself in Romans, chapter 6 and 7. His remarks in these two chapters lead us into the great treasure—house of Romans 8 and the main idea of this chapter.

To those Christians who might surmise that they could continue to live in sin, since freedom from the guilt of sin is now available through the blood of Christ, Paul says, "God forbid" (Romans 6:2). This new relationship with Christ is a relationship that begins with our being united with Christ in baptism (Romans 6:3–5), and it demands that we seek to live our lives without sin. In Romans 6:12–14, we read: "Let not sin therefore reign in your mortal body that you should obey the lusts thereof: neither present your members unto sin as instruments of unrighteousness; but present yourselves unto God as alive from the dead and your members as instruments of righteousness unto God. For sin shall not have dominion over you; for you are not under law, but under grace." Without explaining at this point how he can make such a positive statement as "Sin shall not have dominion (or control) over you," Paul proceeds to tell us why we should seek to commit our lives to Christ as servants of righteousness and forsake forever our allegiance to sin. We are in debt to Christ. He has given us the free gift of eternal life. We are his servants.

To continue in sin means death: eternal separation from God. We cannot be servants of Christ and continue as servants of unrighteousness. We have crucified the old man that allowed sin to rule our lives. "Knowing this, that our old man was crucified with him, that the body of sin might be done away, so we should no longer be in bondage to sin" (Romans 6:6). Now under the system of grace, we commit our lives to the doing if right and refusing to allow sin to control us.

But the question still lingers. How is this possible? How can we keep sin from having dominion over us?

As Paul begins chapter 7, we begin the journey toward the answer to our question. First, it is because we are no longer under the law but now live under grace. "For when we were in the flesh, the sinful passions, which were through the law, wrought in our members brought forth fruit unto death." But now we have been discharged from the law, having died to that wherein we were held so that we serve in newness of the spirit and not in oldness of the letter (Romans 7:5–6). The law taught man that he was a sinner. "For through the law comes the knowledge of sin" (Romans 3:20; also 7:7–8). But the law could not provide the means for his overcoming either the guilt or the domination of sin in his life. However, God in his system of grace provides the way for the fleshly or carnal side of man to be overcome and, thus, to allow man's spiritual, regenerate nature to be free to serve God in righteousness.

In Romans 7:13–23, Paul presents a picture of the struggle that goes on between the flesh and the spirit of man, to rule the life of the man who is attempting to serve God. Under law, any system of law, sin has dominion over man. The law, which his mind approves of, is not capable of overcoming the principle of sin (or the tendency to sin) that rules in his members (note verses 15–23). The spiritual nature wishes to obey the spiritual law, but it is not able because it is incarnate and consequently weakened by the flesh. Sin excites and influences the fleshly nature and, thus, prompts man to break the law. Man has the will to do good, but with the flesh mastering him, he can find no way to accomplish it. Man is hindered by the flesh and, because of it, becomes unable to perform the right, which he desires to do (v. 19). The law of sin (or the tendency to sin) ruling in the flesh prevents him from doing good. Because man's spirit is unable to overcome this weakness of the flesh, he is a captive of sin, and sin has dominion over him (v. 23). Neither the Law of Moses nor any other legislative system can make us free from the law of sin and death, which rules our bodies (Romans 8:3).

All of this is changed when Christ and the system of grace enter the picture. The principle of sin and death (the tendency to sin) is now vanquished by a new and stronger principle: "the law of the Spirit of life in Christ." This principle enables the child of God to be free from the mastery of the flesh and its propensity to sin (Romans 8:2). This "law of the Spirit of life in Christ" encompasses the power of the Spirit of Christ, which leads and strengthens the Christian as He dwells within him. Now the spirit of man no longer resists the impulses of the flesh—unaided, suffering hopeless defeat. He is reinforced by the Holy Spirit, who leads him to victory. The Christian, under grace, is now able to do that which the man under the law could not do (v. 8:3)—that is, to walk after the inward spiritual nature, which desires to do right rather than to walk according to the outward, fleshly nature that lusts to do wrong.

Now we understand how Paul could say so forcefully: "For sin shall not have dominion over you, for you are not under law, but under grace." (Romans 6:14).

Romans 8:2 is sometimes interpreted to mean that "the law of the Spirit of life in Christ" is the Gospel, which frees us from our past sins, doing that which the Law of Moses could not do. However, in this context, Paul is concerned with the control of sin in our daily lives rather than the guilt of sin. He is seeking to show us how we can be successful in becoming servants of righteousness.

As Paul continues to speak about the Spirit in Romans 8, he affirms that the Christian is one in whom the Spirit dwells (v. 11). In fact, if one does not have the Spirit, he does not belong to Christ (v. 9). With the Spirit, man is now able to live in accordance with the ways of the Spirit (v. 5–6). In 8:13, Paul seems to sum up all that he has been saying since chapter 6 when he writes: "For if you live after the flesh, you must die; but if by the Spirit you put to death the deeds of the body, you shall live." The putting to death the deeds of the body was that which the man under the law and without the Spirit could not do but is now able to do because of the Spirit of Christ that dwells within him. As previously noted, a similar thought is expressed by Paul in Ephesians 3:16 where we read: "That he would grant you, according to the riches of his glory, that you may be strengthened with power through his Spirit in the inward man." Also note Philippians 4:13 where Paul writes: "I can do all things in him that strengthens me." If we are led by the Spirit (v. 14), then we are indeed the sons of God. The Spirit certainly leads us into all truth by his Word, but it is by the Spirit's dwelling within us that we are so strengthened to overcome the flesh and become servants of righteousness. Indeed, as the fruits of righteousness (the fruit of the Spirit) are evident in our lives, it is as if the Spirit bears witness to the fact that we are being led by Him and are, in truth, children of God and joint heirs with Christ (v. 16–17).

In Romans 8:26, Paul concludes his remarks about the Holy Spirit by affirming that the Holy Spirit helps us in our weaknesses, and He makes intercession for us. (We will present more about His actions as an intercessor in a later chapter.) With respect to our weaknesses, we are particularly in need of help. We need help in conquering these weaknesses, as Paul has so vividly described in Chapters 7 and 8, but also help in praying for that which is truly best for us. The example of the apostle Paul is a case in point. In 2 Corinthians 12:7–10, Paul writes:

> To keep me from becoming conceited because of these surpassingly great revelations, there was given me a thorn in my flesh, a messenger of Satan, to torment me. Three times, "I pleaded with the Lord to take it away from me." But he said to me, "My grace is sufficient for you, for my power is made perfect in weakness." Therefore I will boast all the more gladly about my weaknesses, so that Christ's power may rest on me. That is why, for Christ's sake, I delight in weaknesses, in insults, in hardships, in persecutions, in difficulties. For when I am weak, then I am strong.

While we cannot identify the thorn with which Paul was afflicted, we do know that he asked for the wrong thing in his prayers. Instead of removing the affliction, as he had requested, God gave him the strength to bear it and be stronger for it. While the "thorn in the flesh" was given to Paul to keep him humble, without God's strength to sustain him, he may well have yielded to the temptation to wallow in self-pity, possibly becoming both unfaithful and unfruitful. However, God supplied both the physical and spiritual strength that Paul needed. In all this, Paul came to realize his dependency upon God. For he wrote: "Wherefore I take pleasure in weaknesses, in injuries, in necessities, in persecutions, in distresses, for Christ's sake: for when I am weak, then I am strong." And again, "Now unto him that is able to do exceedingly, abundantly, above all that we ask or think, according to the power that works in us (Ephesians 3:20).

The Greek word for *help* in Romans 8:26 is interesting. It is found only here and in Luke 10:40 where Martha urges the Lord to tell her sister to help her. It literally means "to take hold with one." It is as if two men were carrying a log, one on each end, thus, helping one another with the load. The Holy Spirit takes hold of our burden and helps us carry it. He provides the strength that we lack in our weakness. He does not only provide us with the spiritual strength we need to resist temptation (Romans 8:2, 13), he also helps us in our petitions to God. This he does by making intercession for us.

One question that may be asked concerning this phase of the Spirit's work is: If the indwelling Spirit strengthens us and enables us to overcome the tendency to sin, why is it that the child of God continues to sin?" How is it that we can be made free from the tendency to sin (Romans 8:2) and still occasionally transgress God's laws? There is no doubt that the indwelling Spirit enables us to overcome temptation and the tendency to sin, but we do not always allow ourselves to be led by the Spirit. By cherishing impure thoughts in our hearts, we may grieve the Spirit or quench the Spirit.

To the degree which the Christian seeks after and obeys God, to that degree he receives the influence of the Spirit. When the Christian hungers and thirsts after righteous-

ness and strives to keep his heart free, he will be strengthened more and more by the Spirit's dwelling within him.
Man has no right to blame God or the Spirit for his sins
if he fails to permit the Spirit to lead him and strengthen
him. In Ephesians 4:30, Paul exhorts us to "grieve not the
Holy Spirit of God," and in 1 Thessalonians 5:19, he again
exhorts us by saying, "Quench not the Spirit." The Christian
is never overwhelmed by the indwelling Spirit so that he is
unable to exercise his freedom of choice. The Holy Spirit
provides our human spirit with that source of strength that
is so necessary for us to overcome the tendency to sin, but
we must allow ourselves to use it.

Swete sums up the relationship of the indwelling Spirit
to the flesh in the following:

> The life of the Spirit, as it proceeds, encounters a
> hostile force which Paul calls the flesh, and the his-
> tory of the Christian life is the history of a lifelong
> war (Galatians 5:17). The flesh is regarded as human
> nature, fallen and sinful, corrupt and morally decay-
> ing; the precise opposite in man of the principle of
> life which is communicated by the Spirit of God.
> In view of this antinomy men fall into two catego-
> ries, those who are in the flesh and those who are in
> the Spirit (Romans 8:5, 8f). In the Christian, as the
> Spirit gains upon the flesh, there grows up within
> the man, the mind of the Spirit, an attitude of
> thought and will which changes the direction of the
> inner life, inclining it to the Divine, and the eternal.
> To live by the Spirit, to talk by the Spirit, this was
> one safeguard against relapsing into the lusts of the
> flesh (Galatians 5:16-18 "So I say, live by the Spirit,
> and you will not gratify the desires of the sinful
> nature. For the sinful nature desires what is contrary

to the Spirit, and the Spirit what is contrary to the sinful nature. They are in conflict with each other, so that you do not do what you want. But if you are led by the Spirit, you are not under law.").[2] Also note Romans 8:14, which states "because those who are led by the Spirit of God are sons of God.

What have we learned about the strengthening power of the Holy Spirit? As Christians, where we once failed, we can now succeed. Why? Because we now have the help of the Holy Spirit.

"I am addicted to drugs/alcohol, and I cannot stop." Oh, yes, you can! "I live with fear—fear of failure, fear of dying, fear of being rejected, fear of being alone. I cannot cease living with fear." Oh, yes, you can! "I can't love those who have hurt me. I can't forgive them." Oh, yes, you can! "I can't control my tongue, my pessimism." Oh, yes, you can! "I can't keep from worrying about my children, or my future, or my health, or my job." Oh, yes, you can! "I can't stop feeling sorry for myself." Oh, yes, you can! "I'm so shy, I wish I could be more outgoing, but every time I try, I do not succeed." Oh, yes, you can! "I wish I could be less selfish and more concerned about others, but I can't change." Oh, yes, you can! "I wish I could be more loving, or kind, or patient, but I can't." Oh, yes, you can! "I wish I could be more joyous, but I lost my husband or my child, and my heart is filled with grief, which I can't get over." Oh, yes, you can! I have a "thorn in the flesh" (These words could refer to a physical pain, an emotional distress, a difficult relationship.) and I don't know if I can bear it much longer? Yes, you can! (For reassurance, read Paul's words in 2 Corinthians, chapter 12, verses 7–10.) "I wish I could sleep better at night and be successful at letting go and turning things over to God, but I never seem able to do it." Oh, yes, you can! I know what's right, and I want to do the right thing, but I end up doing what I don't want to do. My intentions are good, but I always seem to fail." Why? Because you fail to use the power of the Holy Spirit who abides within you when you are a Christian. Yield to the Spirit, let him supply the strength you need to succeed, and you will prevail. Thank God for His precious gift of the Holy Spirit.

But the Spirit is not merely an aggressive force leading the human spirit against the flesh, or a defensive power shielding it from attack. The indwelling Spirit is a constructive power, which builds up a new life within, cooperating with and aiding the spirit of man in the work of bringing the human life to the image of God. "For the life of the Spirit of Christ in the individual believer is the very life of Christ in him, reproducing the character of Christ by forming Christ within his heart" (Galatians 4:19).[3] Christ dwelling in the heart of the Christian through the Spirit becomes the life of our lives. (Galatians 2: 20: "I have been crucified with Christ and I no longer live, but Christ lives in me. The life I live in the body I live by faith in the Son of God, who loved me and gave himself for me.") Thus, the inner life of man is strengthened and enriched, until at last it is filled unto all the fullness of God (Ephesians 3:19).

He now has a life that is known by the fruit of his holy life, bearing the fruit of the Spirit. (Galatians 5:22–23: "But the fruit of the Spirit is love, joy, peace, patience, kindness, goodness, faithfulness, meekness and self-control. Against such things there is no law.") What does this man look like, this man who is full of the Spirit (Acts 6:3)? Paul describes him as a man full of love for God and for others. He is unselfish. His life is characterized by acts of kindness and goodness. He is patient and long-suffering. He is not easily angered. He considers others before himself. His attitude is one of joy. Even in times of despair, his heart is still filled with joy because of his relationship with God and Christ through the Holy Spirit. He is at peace with God because he knows he is forgiven through the blood of Jesus. He lives at peace with others as much as it is possible on his part. He is at peace within himself. He does not live with fear—fear of failure, fear of rejection, fear of death, or any other fear. He enjoys inner peace that surpasses all understanding. He is loyal to others, but, above all, he is loyal to God. He is faithful to his commitments. He has a spirit of meekness, which means he possesses a yielding attitude.

In other words, he yields to God in all that God asks of him. He yields to others but never allows himself to be an enabler. He seeks the best for others. He gives others the benefit of the doubt and puts the best connotation on the things he observes. He keeps no record of other people's wrongs. He is quick to forgive. He does not hold grudges or resentment. He controls his tongue and his passions. He does not gossip nor lie. He never uses God's name in vain. He has a servant spirit. He delights in serving others. He seeks to do unto others as he would like for others to do unto him. Jesus is his hero, and he seeks to imitate him in every way. Does such a person exist? Absolutely—but not to perfection, of course.

The characteristics described above are the goals of a spiritual man. Spiritual growth (sanctification) is a process, a lifelong journey—that is, man's quest. Could such a person exist without divine help? Absolutely not! That is the work of the Holy Spirit, who lives in us as Christians to help us achieve the spiritual qualities described above. If we have our minds set on the things of the Spirit, we shall succeed.

> Those who live according to the sinful nature have their minds set on what that nature desires; but those who live in accordance with the Spirit have their minds set on what the Spirit desires. The mind of sinful man is death, but the mind controlled by the Spirit is life and peace; the sinful mind is hostile to God, it does not submit to God's law, nor can it do so. Those controlled by the sinful nature cannot please God. You, however, are controlled not by the sinful nature, but by the Spirit, if the Spirit of God lives in you. And, if anyone does not have the Spirit of Christ, he does not belong to Christ.
>
> Romans 8:5-9

ADDENDUM

Note the verses listed below found in the New Testament that connect power or strength to the Holy Spirit. Some of these verses use the name God instead of the name Holy Spirit, but in the Christian Age, we have already seen that God uses the Holy Spirit (also God) to carry out His purposes and will.

The Power of the Spirit:

Acts 1:8 "But you will receive power when the Holy Spirit comes on you; and you will be my witnesses in Jerusalem, and in all Judea and Samaria, and to the ends of the earth."

Acts 4:33 With great power the apostles continued to testify to the resurrection of the Lord Jesus, and much grace was upon them all."

Acts 6:8 "Now Stephen, a man full of God's grace and power, did great wonders and miraculous signs among the people."

Acts 10:38 "how God anointed Jesus of Nazareth with the Holy Spirit and power, and how he went around doing good and healing all who were under the power of the devil because God was with him.

Romans 1:16 "I am not ashamed of the gospel, because it is the power of God for the salvation of everyone who believes: first for the Jew, then for the Gentile."

Romans 15:13 "May the God of hope fill you with all joy and peace as you trust in him, so that you may overflow with hopes by the power of the Holy Spirit."

Romans 15:19 "by the power of signs and miracles, through the power of the Spirit. So from Jerusalem all the way around to Illyricum, I have fully proclaimed the gospel of Christ."

I Corinthians 1:18 "For the message of the cross is foolishness to those who are perishing, but to us who are being saved, it is the power of God."

I Corinthians 2:4 "My message and my preaching were not with wise and persuasive words, but with a demonstration of the Spirit's power."

I Corinthians 2:5 "so that your faith might not rest on men's wisdom, but on God's power."

I Corinthians 4:20 "For the kingdom of God is not a matter of talk, but of power."

I Corinthians 5:4 "When you are assembled in the name of our Lord Jesus and I am with you in spirit, and the power of our Lord Jesus is present."

I Corinthians 6:14 "By his power God raised the Lord from the dead, and he will raise us also."

II Corinthians 4:7 "But we have this treasure in jars of clay to show that this all-surpassing power is from God and not from us."

II Corinthians 6:7 "in truthful speech and in the power of God; with weapons of righteousness in the right hand and in the left…"

II Corinthians 10:4 "The weapons we fight with are not the weapons of the world. On the contrary, they have divine power to demolish srongholds."

II Corinthians 12:9 "But he said to me, 'My grace is sufficient for you, for my power is made perfect in weakness.' Therefore I will boast all the more gladly about my weaknesses, so that Christ's power may rest on me."

II Corinthians 13:4 "For to be sure, he was crucified in weakness, yet he lives by God's power. Likewise, we are weak in him, yet by God's power we will live with him to serve you."

Ephesians 1:19 "…and his incomparably great power for us who believe."

Ephesians 3:16 "I pray that out of his glorious riches he may strengthen you with power through his Spirit in your inner being."

Ephesians 3:18 "…may have power, together with all the saints, to grasp how wide and long and high and deep is the love of Christ."

Ephesians 3:20 "Now to him who is able to do immeasurably more than all we ask or imagine, according to his power that is at work within us."

Philippians 4:13 "I can do everything through him who gives me strength."

Colossians 1:11 "…and you have been given fullness in Christ, who is the head over every power and authority."

I Thessalonians "…because our gospel came to you not simply with words, but also with power, with the Holy Spirit and with deep conviction. You know how we lived among you for your sake."

II Thessalonians 1:11 "With this in mind, we constantly pray for you, that our God may count you worthy of his calling, and that by his power he may fulfill every good purpose of yours and every act prompted by your faith."

I Timothy 1:12 "I thank Christ Jesus our Lord, who has given me strength, that he considered me faithful, appointing me to his service."

II Timothy 1:8 "So do not be ashamed to testify about our Lord, or ashamed of me his prisoner. But join with me in suffering for the gospel, by the power of God."

II Timothy 3:5 "…having a form of godliness but denying its power. Have nothing to do with them."

II Timothy 4:17 "But the Lord stood at my side and gave me strength, so that through me the message might be fully proclaimed and all the Gentiles might hear it. And I was delivered from the lion's mouth."

I Peter 1:5 "…who through faith are shielded by God's power until the coming of the salvation that is ready to be revealed in the last time."

I Peter 4:11 "If anyone speaks, he should do it as one speaking the very words of God. If anyone serves, he should do it with the strength God provides, so that in all things God may be praised from Jesus Christ. To him be the glory and the power for ever and ever. Amen."

Some of the verses make reference to the action of the Spirit through miraculous gifts and others through his work as He himself abides in every Christian. By *miraculous*, I mean an action by God where the natural laws of physics, chemistry, life, or learning are suspended. Examples of miraculous gifts are: Jesus walking on water, turning water into wine, raising the dead, Moses parting the waters of the Red Sea, the apostles speaking in languages they had not learned, healing the sick, lame, and blind, Jesus passing through a wall, the Holy Spirit guiding men to speak or write information that can come only from God as well as many other actions seen in the life of Jesus and the apostles. Other actions by God and the Holy Spirit are seen in our daily lives. God provides us food, water, air, healing by our bodies' immune system, knowledge available through His Word and wisdom available through prayer (James 1:3), his answering our prayers on a daily basis, his forgiving us through the blood of Jesus, the daily activity of the Holy Spirit as he dwells within us, and the Holy Spirit's interceding in our behalf before the Father.

Whether it is God's action in our behalf in an extraordinary way (the miraculous) or doing what He does for us day after day, these are actions that reflect God's power. While the miraculous actions may be more spectacular than the ordinary everyday work of God (at times through the Holy Spirit), it is no less the power of God. All these actions are that which could not be accomplished by man alone. God's power is God's power!

One final observation, Romans 8:11 reads, "And if the Spirit of Him who raised Jesus from the dead is living in you, He who raised Christ from the dead will also give life to your mortal bodies through His Spirit, who lives in you." The Holy Spirit with his divine power raised Jesus from the dead, and this same Spirit with the same power abides in every Christian to assist him in living his life to the full, bearing the fruit of the Holy Spirit and honoring the heavenly Father.

12

ACCESSING THE POWER OF THE HOLY SPIRIT

THE INDWELLING SPIRIT abides in us to empower us to make right choices. If we have knowledge of His Word, we know what the right choices are. Much of the time, right choices are easy for us to make. Our minds and hearts are already set on doing what God asks us to do or refraining from doing. However, a problem arises when Satan tempts us in areas where we are more concerned about what we want than what God desires.

Be assured that Satan knows where we are most vulnerable. It is in these areas that we need divine help in making the right choice and carrying it out. The problem is more difficult when we are addicted to a particular sin or sins: using drugs; practicing immorality (the works of the flesh (Galatians 5:19–21), misuse of the tongue (gossip, slander, profanity, lying), failing to forgive when we have been hurt, impatience (easily angered), showing indifference to the needs of others. In many instances, other temptations devised by Satan to lead us into sin are less direct and more subtle. For example, when considering the fruit of the Spirit, those characteristics cannot be developed without our being tested or challenged. One cannot grow in patience, love, joy, self-control, etc., without being tempted to do the opposite. Resisting the temptation to sin and obeying instead God's direction lead to growth and maturity in that spiritual characteristic. Satan is also a master in persuading us to simply procrastinate in doing a righteous act; when we postpone taking an action today, we may never respond to that same opportunity, and excuses come easy. "I'm just too busy. I have too much on my plate right now. Others can/will take care of the task." In the situations described above, the help of the Holy Spirit is imperative. May I suggest four steps to help access the power of the Holy Spirit?

First, it is essential that we have our "mind set" on the things of the Spirit. Characteristics of the man filled with the Spirit were described in the previous chapter of this book. Remember the passage in Romans 8:5, which tells us: "Those who live according to the sinful nature have their minds set on what that nature desires; but those who live in accordance with the Spirit have their minds set on what the Spirit desires." A "mind set" means to desire, to focus on, and to commit to achieving that goal. In fact, we can "quench the Spirit." ("Do not put out the Spirit's fire.") We are motivated to have a proper mindset by being in love with God and being grateful for every blessing from Him, as mentioned in Chapter 1. We are also motivated by realizing the consequences of sin.

Second, we recognize the need for God's help in our battle with Satan and sin. This battle cannot be won by our own willpower, our own efforts. When addicted to our sin(s), we cannot prevail without God's help. That help is provided by the Indwelling Spirit. It is much like recognizing that forgiveness of sins is not obtained by our own efforts or by doing more good than evil. We need a Savior, and we have one in Jesus Christ. We owe a debt (the penalty for our sins), which we cannot pay. Christ paid a debt He did not owe (his death for our sins by dying on the cross). In other words, we need an attitude of humility, an attitude that says, "God, I need your help. I cannot do it by myself." The Lord taught, "He who exalts himself with be humbled and he who humbles himself will be exalted (Matthew 23:12). The Holy Spirit cannot provide us the strength we need until we acknowledge we are dependent on him for that help.

Third, we must have a willingness to yield to the Holy Spirit's power. We must have meekness in our lives. In Scripture, meekness does not mean timidity but an attitude of yielding or submitting to God, both to His will and to His strength (power). The Holy Spirit does not force or compel us to accept his power. We, ourselves, can quench the Spirit (1 Thessalonians 5:19).

Fourth, we pray. We humbly pray for the Spirit to help us resist the temptation(s) that Satan has placed before us. Pray, as Paul prayed in Ephesians 3:16. Paul asked that "we might be strengthened by the Holy Spirit in the inner man. Paul's final words in that prayer are "Now to him who is able to do immeasurably more than all we ask or imagine, according to his power that is at work within us…" (Ephesians 3:20). The Spirit helps us do the unimaginable if we trust Him.

Remember the words of Jesus that the Holy Spirit will be given to all who ask the Father. "If you then, though you are evil, know how to give good gifts to your children, how much more will your Father in heaven give the Holy Spirit to those who ask him!" (Luke 11:13).

You may be familiar with the hormone adrenalin produced by the adrenal gland in our bodies. Adrenalin can provide unbelievable strength in our bodies at a moment of crisis. No doubt, you have heard amazing stories about a parent lifting a car off an injured child. Or the story of four American soldiers during the Vietnam war, who came under enemy fire while on a one-lane trail and picked up their jeep by the bumpers and turned it around so they could flee to safety. Such incidents of strength are explained by physicians as an example of the effect adrenalin in the bloodstream can have on the human body.

I suggest the power of the Holy Spirit that is within us is our "spiritual adrenalin." In this case, it is not physical strength provided but spiritual strength. Physical strength is provided by adrenalin at a moment of crisis. Spiritual strength is provided when we are face-to-face with Satan and his attempt to lead us into disobeying God. By the power of the Holy Spirit within us, we can prevail and say, as did Jesus, "Get behind me, Satan."

13

THE HOLY SPIRIT MAKES INTERCESSION

ANOTHER WORK OF the indwelling Spirit is set forth by the apostle Paul in Romans 8:26-27.

> And in like manner the Spirit also helps our weakness: for we know not how to pray as we ought; but the Spirit himself makes intercession for us with groanings which cannot be uttered, and he that searches the hearts knows what is the mind of the Spirit, because he makes intercession for the saints according to the will of God.

"The Holy Spirit is seen here in His most intimate relation with the human consciousness, distinct from it, yet closely associated with its imperfectly formed longings after righteousness, acting as an intercessor on its behalf in the sight of God, even as the glorified Christ does, however not in heaven but in the hearts of believers."[1] Paul does not mean that the Christian does not know how to pray but implies that he needs help in his prayers. To intercede implies intervention on another's behalf. An intercessor is an advocate, one who pleads another's case. This word should not be confused with the word *mediator*. A mediator is one who represents two estranged parties and works to bring about a reconciliation of those two parties. Christ is a mediator; in fact, he is our only mediator (1 Timothy 2:5). Christ is an apostle, one sent from God and representing God. He is also a High Priest, and in this represents man. (Note Hebrews 3:1.) He seeks to bring about a reconciliation between God and man. This he has accomplished through the cross. "And might reconcile them both in one body unto God through the cross, having slain the enmity thereby" (Ephesians 2:16). Christ alone then qualifies as our mediator. However, we have a number of intercessors. We are taught to intercede for one another before the throne of God (1 Timothy 2:1). Christ, who even now is at the right hand of God, makes intercession for us (Romans 8:34; Hebrews 7:25). He is an advocate, taking our petions before the Father (1 John 2:1). The Holy Spirit is also an advocate. "And I will pray the Father and he shall give you another advocate, that he may be with you forever, even the Spirit of truth: whom the world cannot receive; for it beholds him not, neither knows him: you know him; for he abides with you, and shall be in you" (John 14:16–27). The Holy Spirit, even as Christ, makes intercession for us. This the Spirit accomplishes in connection with groanings that cannot be uttered.

The word *groanings* in verse 26 seems to have reference to "the yearning of the human soul after something as yet unrealized." This is how the word is used in verse 22 and 23. Just as the woman groans in the giving of birth, so all creation agonizes, anticipating the birth of a new heaven and new earth. In like manner, we also groan within ourselves, anxiously yearning for the redemption of our bodies (v. 23). The groanings of verse 26 would appear to mean our yearning for deliverance from the weaknesses of the flesh.

While absolute deliverance cannot be a reality until the coming of death or until we receive our spiritual bodies, we, nevertheless, are given now the strength and help that we need in order to present ourselves as instruments of righteousness unto God. Note again the case of the apostle Paul in 2 Corinthians 12 as he yearned for the removal of the "thorn in his flesh." Instead, he was given the strength to endure and to serve. It is the Spirit that takes our inarticulate longings, forming and directing them so as to give them intelligibility and to make them express our own true wants and needs. Then God, who searches and examines our hearts, knows the content and the intent of the intercession. It has been made clear by the Spirit who dwells within us. Who would better know our deepest longings and yearnings than the one sent from God to abide and dwell within our hearts (Romans 5:5; 1 Corinthians 6:19). Not only does the Spirit make our needs known, but he does so in accordance with God's will. As in the case of Paul, we may not know God's will, but the Spirit does. We can be assured that his intercessions, though stemming from our own longings, will always be in harmony with God's will for us. For the Spirit knows not only our hearts but also the mind of God as well. "So the things of God, none knows, except the Spirit of God" (1 Corinthians 2:11).

In all of this, we perceive of God's being active in behalf of man in order that man might be victorious over both the guilt and domination of sin. Such a victory means not only everlasting life but a life that even now reflects the power and might of God as seen in the fruit of holy and righteous service. We see God in Christ as our redeemer and justifier, and as one who makes intercession for us at the right hand of God. We see God in the Spirit as one who leads and guides us into all truth through his Word and who strengthens us by his power in the inward man so that we are able to overcome the weakness of the flesh. The Spirit helps us in our weakness. He conveys to the mind of God our deepest needs and longings and always in accordance with His will. The end result of such divine aid is a life expressed by love, joy, peace, patience, kindness, goodness, faithfulness, meekness, and self-control: the glorious fruit of the Spirit. "In all these things, we are more than conquerors through Him who loved us" (Romans 8:37).

APPENDIX

THE ERROR OF DENYING THE INDWELLING SPIRIT

IT IS ALMOST impossible to study any phase of the Holy Spirit's activities without noticing that certain errors are taught, which are contrary to the teaching of God's Word. This is definitely true concerning the work of the Holy Spirit in the life of the Christian. In this appendix, we will discuss the belief that the Holy Spirit works for the Christian only through the written Word.

Over the past century, several Christian authors have taken the position that the Holy Spirit exerts no influence upon man at any time or in any way, except through the agency of the Word. Believing and teaching that the Holy Spirit operates in conversion only through the Word, they also argue that the Holy Spirit dwells in the Christian only through the Word. This was the position taken by Alexander Campbell in the Rice-Campbell debate. Campbell tried to sustain his proposition from arguments drawn from John Locke's (1632–1704) philosophy, from which it is shown that the nature of man is such that he can be influenced only through words.[1]

However, in Campbell's "Christian System," there are indications that Campbell later in life recognized an influence of the Spirit in sanctification, which could not be explained by Locke's philosophy. Paul says that God has saved us by the bath of regeneration and the renewing of the Holy Spirit, which he poured on us richly through Jesus Christ our Savior (Titus 3:5). This pouring out of the influences, this renewing of the Holy Spirit, is as necessary as the bath of regeneration to the salvation of the soul and to the enjoyment of the hope of heaven. In the kingdom into which we are born of water, the Holy Spirit is as the atmosphere in the kingdom of nature; we mean that the influences of the Holy Spirit are as necessary to the new life as the atmosphere is to our animal life in the kingdom of nature. All that is done in us before regeneration, God our Father effects by the Word or the gospel as dictated and confirmed by his Holy Spirit. But after we are, thus, begotten and born by the Spirit of God—after our new birth—the Holy Spirit is shed on us richly through Jesus Christ our Savior of which the peace of mind, the love, the joy, and the hope of the regenerate is full proof; for these are among the promised fruits of the Holy Spirit.[2]

Campbell does not try to define the method of the Holy Spirit's operating on the Christian, but it is clearly distinguished from the influence of the Spirit through the Word. "It seems evident that Campbell forsook his system at this point and stated religious truth, ignoring the fact that it could not be logically coordinated with his system."[3]

Others, however, fear that to admit that the Holy Spirit works in the Christian in some way other than through the Word is to admit that the Holy Spirit may operate also in man's conversion outside of the Word.

If it can be shown that the divine Spirit works by a direct impact in strengthening the Christian and helping his infirmities, it can never be proven that He does not work in the same way in the conversion of sinners.[4]

Because of this fear, they have denied the work of the indwelling Spirit and claimed that whatever the Spirit does for the Christian is done only through the instrumentality of the written Word. Those who take the above position defend it by two major lines of reasoning. First, they say it is impossible to give any tangible evidence that the Holy Spirit dwells within the Christian, and, if one can have it and never know, of what use is it? Can it be that, having it (the indwelling Spirit) in constant possession since the day of our salvation, we, nevertheless, can give no tangible evidence thereof? Did we know the moment the gift came, and were we conscious of the reception? Who will dare say yes? Who can honestly and intelligently confess to a consciousness of its abiding presence? If one can have it and never know it, of what use is it?[5]

A second argument made is that there is no need for a personal indwelling Spirit because everything that is claimed to be affected by the personal indwelling of the Spirit is clearly accomplished by the Spirit acting through the Word of God. Those passages, which promise the Christian the Holy Spirit and declare the Spirit abides in him, are said to be totally fulfilled as the Christian lets God's Word, which the Spirit inspired, come into his heart.

The holy Scriptures are the only means that the Holy Spirit uses to enlighten the minds of men in regard to every relation they may sustain to God and to comfort and strengthen the heart of the Christian. And the evident reason why the Scriptures are the only means, which the Spirit uses for this object, is the fact that they contain all that God has to say to man, whether he be a sinner or a saint, and that they contain all the motives, considerations, hopes, and fears that can arouse, strengthen, and comfort the heart.[6]

Thus, there is no need for the Spirit's actually dwelling in the Christian since all is accomplished through the written Word. From our study in the preceding chapters, it is clear that the Holy Spirit is promised to the Christian and dwells within him. It is granted that there is mystery connected with how the Spirit dwells within us. But there is also mystery as to how our own spirits dwell in our bodies. Just as it is impossible to explain the workings of our own spirit, it is also impossible to define, or even fully understand, the means and methods of the indwelling Spirit. Although we do not profess to know all mysteries connected with the indwelling of the Holy Spirit, we, nevertheless, can be certain that He dwells within the Christian. The Christian can know that the Holy Spirit dwells within him as certainly as he knows that his sins have been pardoned. He has no "tangible" evidence that he has received the remission of his sins, nor is he actually conscious of his pardon, although he knows from the Bible that if he has obeyed God, he has received the promise of remission of sins (Acts 2:38).

In a like manner, the Christian knows that if he obeys God, he will receive the gift of the Holy Spirit (Acts 2:38, 5:32). The indwelling presence of the Holy Spirit is a matter of faith with the Christian just as is the knowledge of his pardon. It is not a matter of feelings any more than the knowledge of our being pardoned is based on feelings. The criterion is God's Word in both instances, not feelings. If God says that his Spirit dwells within us, then we believe that He does. Also, as the Christian's life bears the fruit of the Spirit, this is evidence that the Spirit abides in him. The fruit of a holy life as evidenced in the Christian is proof that he is being led by the Spirit (Romans 8:14) both through the written Word and the indwelling of the Spirit. "That the Holy Spirit dwells in the Christian is not contradictive of reason. It is only above it and therefore not to be judged by it."[7]

The argument that there isn't any work that the indwelling Spirit could perform that isn't done by the Spirit's acting through the Word plainly contradicts the teaching of the New Testament. Previous lessons have been devoted to showing that the indwelling Spirit comforts, strengthens, and makes intercession for the child of God. In each case, it is a work that can only be accomplished by the indwelling Spirit. It cannot be a comfort to the Christian that God and Christ dwell in him through the Holy Spirit, unless there is an actual indwelling of the Spirit. If God, Christ, and the Holy Spirit all dwell in the Christian only through the Word, what is the point of John's statements in 1 John 3:24 and 1 John 4:13, where he tells us that we know that God abides in us because he has given His Spirit unto us? The impact of this promise as well as its significance is eliminated, unless the Holy Spirit dwells within us personally.

The Word of God cannot be a proof of sonship. It is true that every man who is adopted into the family of God must be taught by the Spirit through the Word before he is adopted, but Paul says that the Spirit is given to him because he is a son, not to prepare him for adoption or to enable him to become a son (Galatians 4:6). "If the reception of the word of truth is all that is meant by the reception of the Spirit, then Paul's rule is reversed and every man receives the Spirit, not because he is a son but that he may become one."[8] The Spirit cannot "seal" the Christian through the Word nor can the Word be an earnest of the Christian's future inheritance. In both cases, the work of the Spirit is accomplished after one has heard and believed the gospel after he has become a Christian (Ephesians 1:13–14). The Spirit was given after they were instructed in and obeyed the Gospel and, hence, is something more than just receiving the Word of God. If the Word of God and one's adherence to it could be proof of sonship, a seal, or sign of covenant relationship and an earnest payment of a future inheritance, then why did it not serve as such under the old covenant?

The Holy Spirit who was the author of the Old Testament just as surely as He is the author of the New Testament bears a different relationship to the Christian than He did to the faithful Jew. This is evident from John 7:39 and Acts 2:38. Those faithful under the old covenant did not possess the Holy Spirit in the same way that the Christian receives Him. Yet, if the Holy Spirit dwells within the Christian only through the written Word, then of necessity the Holy Spirit would maintain the same relationship to the faithful Jew as He does now to the faithful Christian.

To affirm this is absurd in light of the New Testament Scriptures. Where in the Old Testament does it affirm that the Holy Spirit was given to the Jew to prove his sonship, to seal him, or to give him an earnest pledge on an unfulfilled promise? Why did God demand that the Jews be circumcised as a sign or seal of a covenant relationship between God and them if their loyalty to the Word of God, the work of the Spirit, would serve as such a seal? If one's loyalty and adherence to the Word of God today is the seal, why was it not under the old covenant? God has given us the Holy Spirit as a seal or sign of our covenant relationship with him.

But this seal is the personal indwelling of the Holy Spirit Himself. This gift guarantees our sonship and is the downpayment on our future inheritance—eternal life. The strengthening of the inner man (Ephesians 3:16) by the indwelling Spirit is a work that cannot be completely accomplished by the Holy Spirit through the Word. It is only through the help of the indwelling Spirit that man is able to overcome the flesh and the tendency to sin. If the words of the Spirit could fully achieve this end, why weren't the Jews able to overcome the flesh since the Old Testament is also the Spirit-inspired Word? This work of the Spirit, more than any other, shows that the indwelling Spirit performs a work that cannot be accomplished through the written Word alone.

The significance of Paul's basic point in Romans 7 and 8 is nullified, unless the Holy Spirit strengthens us in the inner man so that we are able to overcome the tendency to sin and the deeds of the flesh (Romans 8:2, 3, 13). To deny the personal indwelling of the Holy Spirit is to deny one of the Christian's greatest blessings. It is also to deny a source of strength that is so absolutely necessary in living the Christian life. It is basically this promise that makes the Christian different from the man who lived under the law (Romans 7:15–23). The Christian is now able to live as God would have him to live because he possesses the indwelling of the Holy Spirit.

Another work of the Spirit that obviously cannot be accomplished through the Word is His work as an intercessor. The Word cannot pray for the child of God nor can the Word know his needs and weaknesses. This work can be achieved only by the personal indwelling Spirit.

Let us continue with the line of reasoning of those who do not believe in a personal indwelling of the Holy Spirit. If those passages, which promise the Holy Spirit to the Christian and teach that the Spirit dwells in him, are fulfilled by the Spirit through the Word of God alone, then how does the Holy Spirit maintain a relationship to the Christian different from that which he sustains to the unbeliever? Both possess the Word and both may have a thorough knowledge of it. What is the meaning and purpose of Peter's promise of the gift of the Holy Spirit (Acts 2:38) if it is nothing more than the Word of God? A man must have the Word in his heart before he is saved. If the gift of the Holy Spirit is the Word, then man must receive it before his conversion instead of after his obedience to the gospel as Peter promised (Acts 2:38).

The gift of the Holy Spirit is the Spirit Himself and not merely the written Word. This thought is also brought out by Jesus, "But this spoke he of the Spirit, which they that believed on him were to receive: for the Spirit was not yet given: because Jesus was not yet glorified" (John 7:39). This passage clearly shows that the believer did not possess the Holy Spirit until after the new covenant has established. Therefore, this could not have reference to the written Word, for the Spirit had already operated on the minds of both Jews and Patriarchs through the word. The gift of the Holy Spirit or the indwelling Spirit is promised only to the obedient child of God. However, if this promise refers only to the Word of God, then anyone with a knowledge of God's Word may possess the promise, even before he has obeyed the commands of God. Hence, Christ refers here (John 7:38-39) to an influence of the Spirit over and above exercising through the Word, which it helps our infirmities (Romans 8:26), strengthens us with of truth, influence, by means of might even unto the inner man (Ephesians 3:16); and enables us to bring forth abundantly in our lives the fruit of the Spirit. (Galatians 5:22–23).[9]

Therefore those who affirm that the Holy Spirit operates only through the instrumentality of the Word must deny the work of the indwelling Spirit as a comforter and as one who strengthens the inner man and who makes intercession for him. They must also deny any distinctive meaning, to the promise of the gift of the Holy Spirit. In so doing, they clearly contradict the teaching of the New Testament on the Holy Spirit. "O! Deliver me from the cold material philosophy, which denies that God has placed within me a comforter and a strengthener."[10]

To conclude, Paul states very emphatically in 2 Timothy 3:1, 5: "But mark this: there will be terrible times in the last days. People will have a form of godliness, but deny its power. Have nothing to do with them."

BIBLIOGRAPHY

Barrett, C. K. *The Holy Spirit and the Gospel Tradition*. London: Society for Promoting Christian Knowledge, 1947.

Boles, H. Leo. *The Holy Spirit*. Nashville: Gospel Advocate Company, 1962.

Brents, T. W. *The Gospel Plan of Salvation*. Nashville: Gospel Advocate Company, 1874.

Campbell, Alexander. *The Cristian System*. Cincinnati: Standard Publishing Company, 1835.

Garrison, J. H. *The Holy Spirit*. St. Louis: Christian Publishing Company, 1905.

Garrison, Winfred E. *Alexander Campbell's Theology*. St. Louis: Christian Publishing Company, 1900.

Gordon, A. J. *The Ministry of the Spirit*. Philadelphia: The Judson Press, 1894.

Kelly, Q. *The New Testament Doctrine of the Holy Spirit*. London: W. H. Broom, 1877.

Lard, Moses E. *Commentary on Paul's Letter to the Romans.* Cincinnati: The Standard Publishing Company, 1875.

Lipscomb, David. *Salvation from Sin.* Nashville: Gospel Advocate Company, 1950.

MacDonald, A. J. *The Holy Spirit.* London: Society for the Promotion of Christian Knowledge, 1944.

McGarvey, J. W. *New Commentary on Acts of Apostles: Volume I.* Cincinnati: The Standard Publishing Company, 1892.

McGarvey, J. W. and Philip Y. Pendleton. *The Standard Bible Commentary.* Cincinnati: The Standard Publishing Company, 1916.

Milligan, Robert. *Scheme of Redemption.* St. Louis: Christian Board of Publication, 1868.

Oglesby, Stuart R. *You and the Holy Spirit.* Richmond: John Knox Press: 1952.

Pierce, Samuel Eyles. *The Gospel of the Spirit.* Grand Rapids: William E. Eardmans Publishing Company, 1955.

Sweeney, Z. T. *The Spirit and the Word.* Cincinnati: The Standard Publishing Company, 1919.

Swete, Henry B. *The Holy Spirit in the New Testament.* London: MacMillan & Company Limited, 1909.

Tophel, Gustave. *The Work of the Holy Spirit in Man.* Chicago: Foundlings Home Print, 1880.

Wizloff, Fredrik. *I Believe in the Holy Spirit.* Minneapolis: Augsburg Publishing House, 1936.

Beckwith, C. A. "Perfectionism," *The New Schaff-Herzog Encyclopedia of Religious Knowledge.* Edited by Samuel M. Jackson, 457. Grand Raids: Baker Book House, 1953.

Mullins, E. Y. "Holy Spirit," *International Standard Bible Encyclopedia,* 1406–1417. Grand Rapids: William B. Eardmans Publishing Company, 1952.

Swete, Henry B. "Holy Spirit, *A Dictionary of the Bible.* Edited by James Hastings, II, 411. New York: Charles Scribner's Sons, 1909.

PERIODICALS

Banister, John H. "What Is the Work of the Indwelling Spirit?" Twentieth Century Christian, XVIII (June 1956), 12–15.

Beatty, James. "The Influence of the Holy Spirit," Lard's Quarterly, III (1866), 395–407.

Christopher, Dr. H. "The Gift of the Holy Spirit," Lard's Quarterly, I (1864), 337–367.

Lard, Moses E. "Spiritual Influence as It Relates to the Christian," Lard's Quarterly, I (1864), 225–2241.

Lard, Moses E. "Review of Sigma on the Gift of the Holy Spirit," Lard's Quarterly, (1865), 92–104.

Lard, Moses E. "The Presence of the Holy Spirit in Christians," Lard's Quarterly, III (1866), 245–252.

Longan, G. W. "The Presence of the Holy Spirit in Christians," Lard's Quarterly, III (1866), 162–177.

Munnell, Thomas. "Review of Dr. Christopher on the Gift of the Holy Spirit," Lard's Quarterly, III (1866), 15–29.

Porter, Curtis. "The Work of the Holy Spirit," Firm Foundation, LIII (February 25, 1936), 3.

Roberts, Luther. "The Gift of the Holy Spirit," Firm Foundation LV (May 3, 1938), 1.

Porter, Sanders J. "The Spirit of Christ," Firm Foundation, LV (May 31, 1938), 1–2.

Woods, Guy. "The Gift of the Holy Spirit #2." Firm Foundation, LV, (March 22, 1938), 2.

Woods, Guy H. "The Gift of the Holy Spirit." Firm Foundation, LV, July 26, 1938), 1.

About the Author

Born November 4, 1929. Married Doris M. Griggs in 1950. They have four children: Candace Killip, Bruce Back, Shari Minton, and Adam Black.

Educational Background

Graduated from the University of Oklahoma in 1951 with a bachelor's degree.

Graduated from Abilene Christian University in 1957 with masters' degree in Bible. The subject of Garth's master's thesis is "The Holy Spirit in the life of the Christian."

Publications

Author of *The Holy Spirit* published by Abilene Christian University Press. Have written articles for *Minister's*

Monthly, *North American Christian*, and *20th Century Christian*. Authored "The Benefit of the Doubt," a chapter in the book *What Lack We Yet?* published by Biblical Research Press.

Churches Where Author Served as Minister

Swans Chapel, Texas (1954–1956)
Kingfisher, Oklahoma (1956–1958)
Rome, New York (1959–1968)
Silver Spring, Maryland (1968–1977)
Bakersfield, California (1977–1995)
Retired as senior minister in 1995.
Continues to be involved in marriage and family counseling.
Teaches Bible classes weekly.

Speaking Engagements

Presented lectures on the Holy Spirit in churches in various states in Oklahoma, Texas, Maryland, New York, New Jersey, California, and Ontario, Canada. Garth has also spoken on this topic at lectureships at Great Lakes Christian College, Oklahoma Christian College, Abilene Christian University, Northeastern Christian College, and Pepperdine University.

Military Service

Served on active duty in the US Army 1951–1954; in the Army Reserve 1954–1962. Graduated from Officer's Candidate School in 1951; completed several courses in the Army Chemical Corps School. Discharged with rank of Captain.

Other Activities

Served on the faculty of Mohawk Valley Community College, Utica, New York, 1962–1968, teaching speech and world history. Served on the board of directors for several organizations.

NOTES

IS THE HOLY SPIRIT GOD?

1. A. J. Gordon, *The Ministry of the Spirit* (Philadelphia: The Judson Press, 1894), p. 25

THE HOLY SPIRIT IN THE NEW TESTAMENT—IN THE CHURCH

1. Henry B. Swete, "Holy Spirit," *A Dictionary of the Bible* (edited by James Hastings; Volume II, New York: Charles Scribner's Sons, 1909,) p. 411.

THE WORK OF THE HOLY SPIRIT IN THE LIFE OF THE CHRISTIAN—HIS PURPOSE

1. Alexander Campbell, *The Christian System* (Cincinnati: Standard Publishing Company), p. 49
2. Ibid.
3. *Ibid.*

THE WORK OF THE HOLY SPIRIT THROUGH THE INSTRUMENTALITY OF THE WRITTEN WORD

1. David Lipscomb, *Salvation from Sin* (Nashville: Gospel Advocate Company) p. 102.

THE GIFT OF THE HOLY SPIRIT

1. J. W. McGarvey, *New Commentary pm Acts of Apostles*, (Volume I; Cincinnati: The Standard Publishing Co, 1892) p. 178.

THE RECEPTION OF THE HOLY SPIRIT BY THE CHRISTIAN

1. Gustave Tophel, *The Work of the Holy Spirit in Man*, trans. George E. Shipman (Chicago: Foundlings Home Print, 1880) p. 32.
2. Robert Milligan, *Scheme of Redemption* (St. Louis: Christian Board of Publication), p. 276.
3. J.H. Garrison, *The Holy Spirit* (St. Louis: Christian Publishing Company, 1905), p. 81.
4. Garrison, *op cit.*, p. 73.

THE WORK OF THE INDWELLING SPIRIT AS A COMFORTER

1. Moses E. Lard, "Review of Sigma on the Gift of the Holy Spirit," *Lard's Quarterly*, II (1865), p. 104.
2. Moses E. Lard, 'Review of Sigma on the Gift of the Holy Spirit," *Lord's Quarterly*, II (1865), 103.
3. Everett Ferguson, "The Seal of the Covenant," *Firm Foundation*, (October 20, 1964), p. 667.

4. Moses E. Lard, *Commentary on Paul's Letter to the Romans* (Cincinnati: The Standard Publishing Company, 1875), p. 266.

5. J. W. McGarvey and Philip Y. Pendleton, *The Standard Commentary* (Cincinnati: Standard Publishing Company, 1916), p. 362.

THE WORK OF THE HOLY SPIRIT AS A SOURCE OF STRENGTH

1. Everett Ferguson, "The Seal of the Covenant," *Firm Foundation*, (October 20, 1964), p. 667.

2. Swete, *op. cit.*, p. 343.

3. *Ibid.*, p. 348.

THE HOLY SPIRIT MAKES INTERCESSION

1. Henry B. Swete, *The Holy Spirit in the New Testament* (London: MacMillan And Company, Limited, 1909), p. 221.

APPENDIX: THE ERROR OF DENYING THE INDWELLING SPIRIT

1. Winfred E. Garrison, *Alexander Campbell's Theology* (St. Louis: Christian Publishing Company, 1900), p. 268.

2. Campbell, *op. cit.*, p. 278.

3. Winfred E. Garrison, *op. cit.*, p. 278.

4. G. W. Longan, "The Presence of the Holy Spirit in Christians," *Lard's Quarterly*, III (1866), 163.

5. Guy Woods, "The Gift of the Holy Spirit," *Firm Foundation*, LV (March 22, 1938), 2.

6. Dr. H. Christopher, "The Gift of the Holy Spirit," *Lord's Quarterly*, I (1864) 353.

7. Lard, "Review of Sigma on the Gift of the Holy Spirit," p. 100.
8. T. W. Brents, *The Gospel Plan of Salvation* (Nashville: Gospel Advocate Company, 1874), p. 642.
9. Robert Milligan, *Scheme of Redemption* (St. Louis: Christian Board of Publication), p. 283.
10. Moses E. Lard, "Spiritual Influence as It Relates to the Christian," *Lard's Quarterly,* I, (1864), 211.

28389199R00093

Made in the USA
San Bernardino, CA
27 December 2015